"In the mid 1970s, when women were leading faithfully and effectively at Willow Creek Community Church, I knew that many people questioned our commitment to gift-based ministry. But I never imagined that many Christians would still be questioning that commitment in the twenty-first century. I'm so glad Jo Saxton chose to embrace her calling to lead—and to share her experience and wisdom in *More Than Enchanting*. Thoughtfully grounded in Scripture, Jo writes from both a global and personal perspective, offering inspiration as well as practical tools for women navigating the complexity of leadership in the church. I highly recommend this book!"

Lynne Hybels, advocate for global engagement, Willow Creek Community Church

"Jo Saxton is a great example of a woman operating in the full power of her God-given identity and gifts. We need many more such people in the church. In writing this book, she not only pens a testimony and gives us good reasons to believe; she also inspires us to do likewise. In Jo's words, 'Women are not an afterthought in God's mind but a central part of his creative plan for the world!'"

Alan and Debra Hirsch, authors of *Untamed* (from the foreword)

"Women are at the heart of every movement; therefore we should take seriously the role we can play today in our families, communities, and churches. This much-needed book can be a tool to champion women in all their giftedness. Jo Saxton has established herself as a leader in a variety of contexts, and she has dedicated herself to empowering women in their leadership journeys. She is the ideal person to teach us how to lean into the influence we each have."

Sandra Maria Van Opstal, author of *The Next Worship*

"I love how Jo Saxton invites, encourages, and inspires women to use their gifts in this book. I've heard time and time again from women that they didn't realize that they had permission, or that they felt like they should let someone else do 'it,' but the church needs all of us—both male and female—living out of the ful'

Lindsey Nobles, chief operating officer a

"Every woman is a queen with her own unique kingdom of influence. Jo Saxton's compelling book not only reminds us as women to invest in our own heart of leadership but to invest in women everywhere."

Shayne Moore, author of *Refuse to Do Nothing* and *Global Soccer Mom*

"In the tradition of Carolyn Custis James, Jo Saxton encourages women to live beyond cultural assumptions and churchy expectations and to live fully into our calling. *More Than Enchanting* is a must-read for women—whether they are secure in their callings or just finding their feet."

Caryn Dahlstrand Rivadeneira, author of *Grumble Hallelujah*

"Saxton has changed the conversation. She has catapulted us beyond the same tired debates, the old unanswerable questions and past paradigms to an unmistakable call to action. Women can no longer sit idly on the sidelines or argumentatively in the halls of debate but must step into their unique calling and work in the kingdom. This book is important for all women who influence—from the family to the marketplace to the church. It is also an important read for the men who lead them and are led by them."

Heather Zempel, author of *Community Is Messy*

"Jo Saxton is a leader, visionary, practitioner, and voice that leaders need to hear. This book is an essential resource for anyone serious about investing in the emerging generation of women leaders."

Brad Lomenick, author and speaker

More Than Enchanting

Breaking Through Barriers to Influence Your World

Jo Saxton

FOREWORD BY *Jenni Catron*

IVP Books

An imprint of InterVarsity Press
Downers Grove, Illinois

InterVarsity Press
P.O. Box 1400, Downers Grove, IL 60515-1426
ivpress.com
email@ivpress.com

Second edition ©2016 by Jo Saxton
Original edition ©2012 by Jo Saxton

InterVarsity Press® is the book-publishing division of InterVarsity Christian Fellowship/USA®, a movement of students and faculty active on campus at hundreds of universities, colleges and schools of nursing in the United States of America, and a member movement of the International Fellowship of Evangelical Students. For information about local and regional activities, write Public Relations Dept., InterVarsity Christian Fellowship/USA, 6400 Schroeder Rd., P.O. Box 7895, Madison, WI 53707-7895, or visit intervarsity.org.

All Scripture quotations, unless otherwise indicated, are taken from the THE HOLY BIBLE, NEW INTERNATIONAL VERSION®, NIV® Copyright © 1973, 1978, 1984, 2011 by Biblica, Inc.™ Used by permission. All rights reserved worldwide.

While all stories in this book are true, some names and identifying information in this book have been changed to protect the privacy of the individuals involved.

Cover design: Cindy Kiple
Images: butterfly silhouette: ©yura123/iStockphoto
*   female silhouette: ©Elisabeth Ansley/Trevillion Images*

ISBN 978-0-8308-4331-2 (print)
ISBN 978-0-8308-9131-3 (digital)

Printed in the United States of America ∞

Library of Congress Cataloging-in-Publication Data
A catalog record for this book is available from the Library of Congress.

P	16	15	14	13	12	11	10	9	8	7	6	5	4	3	2	1
Y	30	29	28	27	26	25	24	23	22	21	20	19	18	17	16	

In memory of Emily May Butterfield

Pioneer, trailblazer and my foster mom.

"Many women have done wonderful things,
but you've outclassed them all!"

Proverbs 31:29

Contents

Foreword

JENNI CATRON

I never set out to be a woman leader. I just wanted to use my gifts for the good of others and the glory of God. As it turns out, one of those gifts is leadership and I happen to be a woman. So here I am: a woman leader.

I didn't give much thought to this label until the first time a couple left our church because I was a woman in a position of leadership. It grieved me. I'm one of those people who always takes disproportionate responsibility for everything and everyone within my sphere of influence. So I felt responsible. "It must be me," I thought. "If only I had led differently, or better." Insert self-loathing, insecurity, and every feeling of inadequacy. That one minor episode (and truly it was quite minor) rocked me and triggered a lack of confidence that plagued my leadership for many more years.

My leadership journey, while certainly challenging at times, has not been as difficult as many of yours. Too often I hear stories from women who have abandoned their leadership gifts because the resistance was just too much. Exhausted and feeling defeated, they have walked away and sidelined their gifts.

Leadership begins with influence, and influence by definition means *the power to change or affect someone*. Think about this for a minute: The power to change or affect someone. This is a huge responsibility! And yet women do this every day. Mothers, wives, sisters, and friends—we as women have tremendous affect on the lives of those around us, but time and again we shrink back from our influence and neglect to develop the budding leadership gifts within us.

More Than Enchanting is a resource I wish I'd had years ago as a young leader. Jo Saxton is one of those rare leaders who has waded the murky waters of leadership and come through graciously resilient. She understands the fears, doubts, and challenges that plague us women as we peek around the corner to sneak a glimpse of our potential. She believes in us. She believes in God's power to work through us and she has the wisdom to guide us to living out the purpose that God has designed us for.

I'm praying ginormous prayers for you as you read this book. I'm praying that God awakens within you every gift that has lain dormant. I'm praying that the doors swing wide for your influence to flourish. I'm praying that you catch a glimpse of the power and potential of God's work in your life as you embrace your gifts of leadership and passionately use them for the good of others and the glory of God. You were made to influence the world in ways that no one else can, and I'm quite confident that *More Than Enchanting* will be another tool that God uses to bring that influence to life!

Acknowledgments

Chris, my husband and mainstay. Thanks for supporting me, believing in me and encouraging me to fly. To our beautiful, girls, Tia and Zoë. I'm so proud of you and thankful that I get to be your mom.

So many great people have helped with this book. Thanks to Bry, Zan and Lorna, who were lifesavers when my laptop was stolen. Thanks to Blakely Page and Annwen Stone, who contributed to the manuscript with hard work, interviews, input and insights—amazing women! And to all the leaders who agreed to share their stories with honestly and vulnerability, thank you for your contribution.

This book has undertaken quite the journey to reach your hands. My heartfelt thanks to Hodder Faith who first published the book in the UK back in the day, and to the IVP team who first brought it to the US over five years ago. And I'm especially grateful to Helen Lee and the current IVP team for giving this book a second life and the chance to speak to a new audience. It's a precious gift that I don't take for granted. Thanks also to the fabulous Jenni Catron for your wonderful foreword. I love your leadership and vision and I'm grateful for your friendship.

Leadership is challenging sometimes, so it's essential to have people cheering you on from the sidelines, encouraging you to keep going. On the hard days I look up and see that I'm surrounded. I'm thankful for my wider family and closest friends who are only a text away; you bring me to my feet. My thanks to Wendy, Jim and Rose; you are not only great agents, but supportive friends too! Love and thanks to the 3dmovements gang, both the board and the leaders across the movement who are the hands and feet of Jesus in their context daily. And so much love to our church community Mission Point Church, who are our family and inspiration all at once.

I'm also thankful for the fellow women leaders (from every walk of life) who I meet when I'm out there speaking, coaching and consulting. Your courage and example and passion are fuel to my fire.

Yes, I'm surrounded, and my life and call is made richer because of all of you. Thank you all.

Finally I want to honor the One who called me by name, gave me new life and a whole new purpose. To my amazing, wonderful, loving Heavenly Father . . . Thank You.

Introduction

PHENOMENAL WOMAN

Leadership is influence. Nothing more, nothing less.

JOHN MAXWELL

DO YOU KNOW AN INFLUENTIAL WOMAN—a woman who, by her character and actions, changes people's lives? She may not see herself as influential, and probably won't advertise any influence she has. Perhaps, like Aunt May, she's too busy getting on with transforming lives and communities to stop and give herself a definition. But when you look at who she is and what she does, you see a woman shaping the world around her.

Influential women are everywhere. There are the women who've stepped into the highest roles of political leadership in their countries. In recent years we've seen Margaret Thatcher of the United Kingdom (known as the Iron Lady for her style of leadership) and Corazon Aquino and Gloria Arroya of the Philippines lead their respective nations. Benazir Bhutto was the first woman to lead a Muslim state. Other female heads of state include Michele Bachelet of Chile, Ellen Sirleaf of Liberia, Luisa Diogo of Mozambique, Vaira Vike-Freiberga of Latvia, Tarja Halonen of Finland and Mary McAleese of Ireland, and there are others. Forbes has named Germany's chancellor, Angela Merkel, the world's most powerful woman for four consecutive years.

Influential women are not limited to the political sphere either. There have been forty female Nobel Prize winners from 1901 to 2009. Marie Curie, the physicist and chemist, won it twice: the Nobel Prize for Physics in 1903 and for Chemistry in 1911. Other women have received awards for their contributions to the scientific world (most recently Ada E. Yonath), but also in literature, and economics, medicine and world peace. Women have played their part in changing the way we look at the world. Rosa Parks refused to give up her bus seat and became a catalyst in the civil rights movement which would change the face and shape of the United States. Wangari Maathai of Kenya, a Nobel Peace Prize winner and founder of the Green Belt Movement, is known for her commitment to democracy, human rights and environmental conservation.

In the arts and popular culture, female musicians, entertainers, authors and talk show hosts form and inform our worldview. In 2008 the *Daily Telegraph* ran a series of articles naming the fifty most influential Britons in the United States. Far above the titans of industry, finance and technology, lodged at number two was Jo Frost, more commonly known as Supernanny—with a popular TV show and three bestselling books. As the article said, "If 'influence' means the extent to which someone directly changes how others behave, the woman who introduced American parents to the wonders of the 'naughty step' and other non-violent child discipline tactics should be near the top of any such list."[1]

Then of course there's Oprah. More than a talk show host, she's a magazine, a TV network, a book club, a philanthropist, a U.S. presidential candidate endorser—she's almost a way of life! It's said that when she was asked about a possible career in politics, her response was that she'd have less influence that way. And with millions of people tuning in to her shows and buying her magazine, she's got a point.

It's not only women who are public figures who are influential. It's estimated that over 60 percent of the world's farmers are women.

In sub-Saharan Africa that figure rises to about 80 percent, As a result, international bodies have increased their efforts of investing in women. Peter Greer of Hope International (a Christian nonprofit organization seeking to alleviate poverty through microfinance development) notes:

> Women are key in rebuilding communities around the world—and in the developing world, carry a disproportionate amount of the responsibility for family and community well-being. With HOPE, we're currently serving 300,000 entrepreneurs in 14 countries—and 80 percent of them are women. A woman is the heart of the home. It's more likely that when you help a woman start or expand a business, a greater percentage of her income will be used for school fees, nutrition, housing improvements.

In a very different part of the world, *Time* magazine ran a feature called "The Rise of the Sheconomy." It noted that in the United States, the increasing earning power of women was causing businesses to change the way they operated in order to attract the powerful female consumer. Furthermore, in the United States, women have control over 51.3 percent of the nation's private wealth. The article noted that such was the growing economic influence of women globally that studies now viewed women as the next emerging economy.[2]

All over the world, in education, in schools, in homes, in shops and offices, influential women are everywhere. Some are married, some are single, some are parents, and some are not. They're young; they're senior citizens. They're every shape, size and color, and they're found in every strata of society. Such women are incredibly inspiring! I wonder if you see them in your family, among your friends, at work.

I wonder if you see an influential woman when you look in the mirror.

INFLUENTIAL CHRISTIAN WOMEN?

As Christians we know we're called to be effective agents of change in society. We recognize that, for all the amazing technological and scientific advances we've made, there are areas where society crumbles, in desperate need of the transformative love and the power of the gospel. A glance at the news around the world and our local community, a walk through our neighborhood, even a glance at the forgotten neighborhoods of our towns can be the salutatory reminder we need. And it's not just the big issues—crime and poverty, corporate greed and injustice—that humanity seems unable to fix using its own resources. A mere hour dealing with the politics of our workplace, or the conflicts within our relationships, reminds us that there's that matter of the human heart that we have yet to resolve.

Jesus describes us as salt and light. Salt, the great preserver, the distinctive flavor, the grit on difficult terrain. Light, exposing the things that hide away in the dark and providing a pathway for safe travel and direction. We're not merely a church building, event or program; we're a body. We're active, called to communicate and incarnate the message of the gospel. We've been commissioned to make disciples who would follow in Jesus' footsteps. As Christian women, all that God has invested in us—our gifts, talents, passion and energy—is to be employed and deployed to see his kingdom come wherever we are. We're ready to take on and change the world, right? Right? Well, not always, not exactly. For many Christian women, this is where it gets confusing, frustrating, even painful. Because despite our incredible capacity to shape the world around us, our talents have not always been recognized, our insights not always received, simply because of our gender. Florence Nightingale, understood today for her role in the Crimean War and as the founder of the modern nursing profession, said this of how her considerable gifts and talents were received within the church:

I would have given her my head, my heart, my hand. She would not have them. She did not know what to do with them. She told me to go back and do crochet in my mother's drawing room; or if I were tired of that to marry and look well at the head of my husband's table. You may go to the Sunday school if you like it, she said. But she gave me no training even for that. She gave me neither work to do for her nor education for it.[3]

Sadly her experience is not unique; it echoes through the ages.

ONE MOMENTOUS NIGHT

A number of years ago I was speaking at an evening gathering at Momentum, a festival for twentysomethings. The talk looked at John 13, where Jesus washes the disciples' feet, and explored our call as believers to serve one another and wash the feet of a broken world. At one point I mentioned in passing that this call was for everyone, both men and women. It's customary at Momentum that, at the end of the talk, people are given an opportunity to respond to what they've heard and receive prayer. Mike Pilavachi (who led the meeting) and I both sensed that on this occasion, among other things, it was appropriate to raise the issue of women in leadership and offer prayer for women who'd experienced hurt, rejection or frustration in the area of leadership on account of their gender. While on the inside I was sure it was the right thing to say, to be honest I felt uncomfortable. I'd led seminars and workshops on women in leadership, but I'd never simply mentioned it from the main stage before *while talking about something else.* I hoped it didn't look as though I was standing on my own personal soapbox.

My thoughts and insecurities were interrupted as I noticed young women start to make their way to the front for prayer. There were so many of them—it was as though they appeared out of nowhere and just kept on coming to the front, many with tears streaming down their faces. It was unsettling to watch. Silent tears turned to stifled sobs, then for some the sobbing grew louder; for a few it turned to wailing. It was hard to listen to. Mike asked for the ministry team to come forward, but a number of them were already at the front, waiting for someone to pray with them. And weeping. The atmosphere was edgy and raw; a lot of women were finally giving voice to their experiences. It was like listening to a lament.

Mike stepped forward and spoke. "I just feel I need to speak to the men here for a moment. Some of you are wondering if it's all getting a bit carried away. I feel the Lord is saying in response. 'You have no idea what these women have been through.'" We prayed for the women for a while longer and then prayed for both the men and women who felt called to wash the feet of a broken world.

The atmosphere was somber in the leaders' meeting review the following morning. Even though we were glad for the response, one of the speakers summed it up when she said, "I kind of thought we'd come further along than that."

CONVERSATIONS ON THE JOURNEY

How far have you come on your journey in leadership? I wonder what has stood in your way. Lack of encouragement, lack of investment, outright hostility, lack of confidence? That night at Momentum wasn't the first nor the last time I've wiped a female leader's tears as she shared her story. Nonetheless, it's the nature of the conversations (often with groups of women at a time) and the questions that arise that have convinced me that, as a church, we need to pay attention to this subject again. Naturally there are the theological questions that women are asking. But they also want to know what to do with the gifts that God has given them; they ask what godly influence, what *leadership*, looks like in the responsibilities in the workplace, the community, the home and, yes, in the church. Many feel a call that inspires and compels them, but also that isolates or frustrates them. Some want to serve God but feel that their God-given gifts and qualities are more recognized outside the church than within it. Some feel like missionaries in the workplace and community and home without the empowering, supportive commission from their wider church family.

Other women recognize that they need some input on being a woman with influence, but they are unsure where to go to find it. They want to know who God designed them to be and what that could look like. They want to know how the things going on inside, in their hearts and minds, shape the life they lead on the outside. Where do they go to process the loneliness and temptations they face, and how that affects their calling? Where do they admit their struggles with sexual temptation, greed and insecurity? They know that these questions are too intimate to ask male peers and mentors. They see a need for a place where they can be transparent and vulnerable about the challenges of leadership, but how do they do that when they are busy being responsible for everyone else? And where do they go for encouragement and accountability with their calling and passions and big impossible dreams? Who invests in them but also challenges them? Who walks with them on the journey, giving advice and insights on simply how to do it? So many questions.

When we feel we have nowhere to go with this question, it's easy to feel frustrated, disillusioned and distracted. If we don't see other women in churches or communities processing the same questions or even ones a few steps ahead, it's easy to feel lonely. So while our hearts say yes to God, and continue to do so, they remain paralyzed by questions that we simply can't find answers for.

FEELING STUCK? COULD YOU BE CAUGHT IN IMAGINATIVE GRIDLOCK?

Are you stuck? Overwhelmed by the lack of answer and direction and unable to move forward into all that God has for you? In *A Failure of Nerve: Leadership in the Age of the Quick Fix*,[4] the late Edwin Friedman (rabbi, family therapist and leadership coach) used the term "imaginative gridlock" to describe what happens when a person, community or society is stuck, unable to progress into the future. He observed three main characteristics in imaginative gridlock:

- a treadmill of trying harder doing the same old things, hoping for different results

- a focus on new answers to old questions, rather than changing the questions

- polarized either-or, all-or-nothing thinking

When I first heard Friedman's words, I thought of the times when, as a woman in leadership, I've felt trapped in "imaginative gridlock." I'd definitely exhausted myself on that treadmill of trying harder to prove to people (and sometimes myself) that God had called me to lead. I'd certainly debated endlessly with friends and strangers on the age-old question of women in leadership. Interestingly, regardless of whoever won the debates, the answers to the question never seemed to convince anyone nor satisfy. Worse, relationships were bruised and hearts became defensive. I recalled the many occasions when I'd wrestled alone with whether women could or could not lead, whether leadership was a black-and-white choice between marriage and ministry, kids or career. My either-or processing gave no room for creativity or possibility and was heavy on the heart. It was a definite case of imaginative gridlock, and at times it was overwhelming. Has your potential for influence become stuck somewhere, lost in endless questions, buried under uncertainty, perhaps trapped in your own version of imaginative gridlock? If it is, we need to find a way through.

BREAKING THROUGH

It appears that there are many reasons why women are held back from becoming influential in the world around them. But whether the reasons are internal, such as a lack of confidence, "imaginative gridlock" or external limitations on opportunities and investment offered to women, we all pay a huge price when this happens. The

Great Commission that Jesus gave to his disciples is an adventure we all embark on, but it is also a battle, a lifelong call to see the kingdom come on earth. That battle needs both men and women; we can't expect to win a war with half the army absent. Nor will we be as effective if half the army is unsure as to whether they should be there in the first place and are ill equipped for the challenges ahead. It's a battle strategy that's sure to fail. I believe a lack of investment in female leadership isn't just personally frustrating and debilitating; it frustrates and debilitates the bigger cause to which Christians are called. Yes, women suffer, sometimes terribly. But the kingdom— the cause—suffers too.

Loren Cunningham, founder of YWAM, recounted a conversation with Dr. Yonggi Cho, founder and pastor of the Yoido Full Gospel Church, South Korea, the world's largest church:

> He told me about a certain country he had just visited where the work of God has struggled for many years. He said, "All their churches are so little! And all of them are holding back their women not allowing them to do what God calls them to do. I've told them to release their women, but they insist that's not the problem. They ask me, 'What's the key to your church?' I tell them again, 'Release your women,' but they just don't hear me!"[5]

This book doesn't debate whether or not women are called to leadership. While we'll explore theology in places, its intention is not to focus on points of disagreement with some of our brothers and sisters in Christ with whom, outside this topic, we have a lot in common! They're our family. This is a book that recognizes that women already do lead. It acknowledges that we have a huge influence in shaping society as mothers, lovers, spouses, friends, as professionals making significant decisions every day at work, as members of our local communities and, yes, as church leaders. This book sees that many Christian women already have ideas and dreams, visions and strategies to see God's kingdom come on earth. Dreams and visions that the Father gave to his beloved daughters. When we get beyond ourselves and think of the gospel, when we remember the new life that we've received, we know we're called to bring his influence in the situations we face every day. We're called to serve, to love, to hold, to pioneer and speak out, to work and build families and communities in the name of Jesus. We're commissioned to respond in some way, to be someone who will do something. To live influential lives in every way, including as leaders. We can't ignore the power of the gospel we've received to transform the needs of the world around us. We just need to work out where to begin, and how to get ourselves ready to respond to God's call on our lives.

When asked to describe her dreams for Christians in leadership, Captain Danielle Strickland, the Salvation Army's social justice director for the Southern Territory in Australia, stated,

> I'd like to see one hundred percent mobilization, based on giftedness and full on commitment by everyone to the mission field in every community; a full on frontal assault against the enemy. To make that happen I think we all just need to fall in love with Jesus and have a totally reckless abandonment to obeying his voice. I think if we were *really* going into battle we'd stop fussing about things like the women issue. We'd stop looking at who's to the side of us and start looking frontward at the battle, grabbing whoever we're next to and not caring whether they're black, white, male or female! We just need to see more of that. I easily get peeved with these controversies. To me they're peacetime issues, like bureaucracy. When you're trying to fight, it's just not the point.[6]

WHERE DO WE GO FROM HERE?

It's my hope, prayer and passion that this book will not only inspire you but will be a tool that helps you grow and take hold of the sphere of influence God has for you.

Healthy leadership is a bit like an iceberg: only a fraction of it is visible. The broadest understanding of leadership takes our skills, talents and passions, gives them some responsibility and puts them to work. Still, there is so much more to leadership than the activities we see a leader undertake. Much of what matters in a leader's life takes place beneath the surface, in our hearts and our mindsets, or in our lives far away from our actual responsibilities. *It's how we deal with these areas that takes us from a call and desire to lead to becoming a leader with an influential life.*

Like you, I long to see women given more opportunities to realize their God-given call and potential. However, as part of that I want to see women given *all* that they need. We don't just need opportunity; we need the capacity to thrive as leaders—and again that is largely a work that takes place internally. I want to see women given the kind of investment that empowers them so they have energy, capacity and, frankly, desire to be influential leaders throughout their lives. Even through to the beautiful old age of 102! Opportunities and skills development do play a significant role in that. But there are more things to consider, the hidden things such as getting secure in our God-given identity, working out our calling, working on our character, dealing with past hurts. We'll need to reflect on how busy we get and whether it makes us more effective. We'll need to consider our approach to working with other women, as well as working alongside men. We'll need to think about relationships, friendships, accountability. We'll need to understand how different seasons of life shape our leadership, and how to remain open to God and flexible with life throughout it all. We'll need to consider how we keep Jesus at the center of it all. We'll spend most of our time beneath the surface, working through these areas. But we'll still regularly come up for air. Dispersed throughout the book are reflections and advice and top tips from a wide range of leaders, both male and female. Expect their words to sustain you, challenge you and invest in you.

So I hope this book will be a catalyst for your own ideas and thoughts too! There'll be questions for you to reflect on, and recommendations for further study and discovery. Let this book be just the starting point that gets you moving. Interact with it, talk about it, and go viral with it! Get together with friends over coffee, form a book club, challenge and share ideas, dream dreams, make plans and go for it. See where the Father leads you. And let me know the exciting adventures he leads you into.

PUPA TO BUTTERFLY

Some of us reading this book do so wearily, having struggled as women in leadership for some time. We're so tired of the frustration this topic has brought to our lives, we're tempted to walk away. I know we'd like this issue to be clearer and easier. At least, I know I would! I remember a few months ago I felt as if I was constantly learning how to lead as a woman without much of a road map to guide my way, and I was tired of it. I desperately wanted someone to tell me exactly what to do, who to be, how to live, but no one did. So I hid away to be alone with God for a while.

Alone, I told him of my weariness, my loneliness in that moment of confusion. As I prayed, in my mind's eye I saw a picture of a chrysalis, hanging, waiting. I remembered reading somewhere that if you open the chrysalis for the emerging butterfly, it dies. It seems strange: all you are trying to do is set it free, but the butterfly's wings aren't strong enough. The butterfly needs the struggle; it's a vital process even though it's difficult. When the butterfly finally breaks through and emerges from the chrysalis, it will be fully formed and free, but it will also be strong enough to fly. I understood in that moment that I needed the journey more than I needed the road map, no matter how stretching it was. I may have been aching, but I was growing. I may have been hurting, but with him I was healing and learning and getting stronger day by day. The breakthrough would come one day, but when it did I'd probably value the journey much more.

It may be hard, even painful, to look at what it means for you to be an influential woman. It may tap into all kinds of frustrations, memories and wounds. It may feel as though we're in the dark, grasping for the Lord's wisdom. But do it anyway. Discover again who he's called you to be, who he always made you to be. Engage with him on this: it will be a valuable process that will both strengthen and mature you, and ultimately liberate you.

So when you're ready, start to move . . .

Slowly but surely work your way out of the chrysalis. Let God's purposes unfold, spread your wings, look toward the Son and then—fly.

Reflections on Leadership

Kate Smith is married to Duncan. Together they lead a church in North Carolina and oversee a number of ministries in the United States. These are her wise words for women starting out in leadership:

1. *We are born with the potential to lead but have to grow as leaders. Be willing to learn from others and read about leadership. It is important to be aware of your strengths and weaknesses and the areas that you are strong in and the areas you need help and support in. Be willing for spiritual fathers and mothers and mentors to speak into your life. We always need that! Realize that there will always be people around you who are better at leadership or more qualified or experienced than you are.*

2. *If God promotes you into a position of leadership before you feel ready, remember that it is the Lord who establishes you and that this position is not just for you. This position has been given in order that you can influence others and make them great and lead them into kingdom purposes for their life. Remember that Jesus never used his position to use or manipulate anyone but knew what it was like to lay down his life for others, even when they spoke against him or maligned his name. He sees fit that you have the*

potential to grow into this leadership position with his help and the help of those around you.

3. *We must stay connected to the Father who is our source of strength and wisdom. If we don't feed on him as the Word and Drink of the Holy Spirit, we will become dry and weary. If we don't get life from God, then we can never be an inspiration to others. We must develop our secret life with our heavenly Father and grow in intimacy and prayer, learning to rest in him even through the trials of leadership.*

The Blueprint

*Our authenticity, as well as our power, is unleashed
when we live out our true identity and calling in Christ.*

ALAN AND DEB HIRSCH, *UNTAMED*

*It's in Christ that we find out who we are and what we are living for.
Long before we first heard of Christ and got our hopes up, he had his
eye on us, had designs on us for glorious living, part of the overall
purpose he is working out in everything and everyone.*

EPHESIANS 1:11-12 *THE MESSAGE*

I HAD NO IDEA I'D FEEL THIS WAY. How can you feel more
complete when you already have a fulfilled life? How can you become more whole when you didn't know you were broken? Be given
back something you weren't even aware had been taken?

It was February 1999, and I was in Lagos as part of a mission team
from my church. The ministry and mission trip was phenomenal, in-
tense, hectic, inspirational, a story in itself for another time. Needless
to say it changed my life in many ways. However, visiting Nigeria was
something of a personal pilgrimage too. My parents immigrated to
England from Nigeria in the 1960s, so I was going "home." I'd expected it to be personally significant, and it was. I saw my father, and
relatives I'd not seen for years, and was united with cousins I'd never

met. I'd expected those events to be powerful, emotional, wonderful. Yet still something else was happening, something deeper.

Being surrounded by fellow Nigerians and Yorubas, my family's tribe, produced some sort of epiphany, awakening, revelation—I couldn't find the words to explain what was happening to me, enveloping me. But it was enveloping me. On one level, I was just surrounded by people, everyday ordinary people, young, old, rich, poor, men and women. But on another level, I heard the timbre in a woman's voice and it was like mine, the cadence in someone's laughter, like mine. I looked at people and saw mannerisms and movement, the stride, the gait—like mine. It was amazing and at times overwhelming. Had I missed out on this all this time? Would my life, my confidence, my everything have been different had I known *this*—experienced this earlier? How I wished I'd learned Yoruba as a child, rather than grasping at phrases! My thoughts and yearnings dissolved in the warm embrace of the new mothers and fathers, aunties and uncles I'd found. They called me by one of my many Nigerian names, and they asked me to sit with them a while, stay with them a while longer. We only had three weeks.

Just before I left, a pastor asked me if I had enjoyed my visit to Nigeria, to Lagos.

"Yes," I replied, "I feel I've been given a piece of my identity back. A piece that I didn't know I didn't have."

OUR HOMECOMING

As we explore what it means to be an influential woman, perhaps we too need a homecoming. We need to discover the fullness of who we truly are. Contrary to the many mantras of our day, our identity is not found deep within us: it's given. We're shaped by our families, relationships, experiences, communities. We are labeled by the voices of authority figures and media messages that speak compellingly over our lives. Because there are so many competing voices and experiences seeking to label us, we may need to remind ourselves, or even discover for the first time, what God has in mind for us as women. Rising above all other voices and experiences, our Creator has given us an identity. And though humanity walked away from our Creator, at the cross his Son has made the way for our relationship to be restored and for us to rediscover all we were ever meant to be.

It's vital that we understand what that looks like for us. Some women may not feel embraced by the Scriptures; rather, we've felt rejected and alienated by what we've been told our identity is. So when God looked down from heaven and made women, what on earth was he thinking? Seriously, what did he have in mind for us to be and to do? We need to understand it and to embrace it, because our understanding of our identity determines the life that we live.

> Q. As you reflect upon your life, who or what has shaped your identity? Does it affect your understanding of a call to leadership? If so, how?

WILL THE REAL EVE PLEASE STAND UP?

As the first woman God created, Eve inevitably defines who we are. As theologian Carolyn Custis James writes, "God cast the mold for all women when he created Eve. She embodies the secrets of his original blueprint for us. So we rightly turn to her to understand who we are and to discover God's purposes for us."[1]

Eve might well be seen as the most influential woman in history. There's only one problem. The church and culture's tendency throughout history is to view Eve through the lens of her mistake and the Fall. We recall the decision that resulted in humanity's alienation from God that would cost God his only Son to restore. We remember the end of Eden and the start of shame and blame in the garden where no one could take responsibility for either their actions or their inaction. We're perpetually reminded of the devastating schisms in male-female relationships that began on that day. Perhaps there are some glimpses of her true design in some broken pieces that remained, but even they are overshadowed by that choice, that day. Those shadows have extended through history, labeling women as more easily deceived than men, as the temptress. Women are weak-willed and potentially dangerous, so perhaps in fact it's wise and responsibly protective to limit a woman's role? Consequently, women have often been defined and reacted against in response to a fallen Eve instead of the fullness of God's glorious original design. It's as though we have forgotten that there actually was a glorious design before the Fall, that there was an identity given to humanity when God spoke his words of life and love to Adam and Eve. If we want to know our original design and purpose, *then the original Eve is where we need to begin.*

MADE IN HIS IMAGE AND LIKENESS

Then God said, "Let us make human beings in our image, in our likeness. . . .
So God created human beings in his own image,
in the image of God he created them;
male and female he created them.

GENESIS 1:26-27 TNIV

In the early stages of church history, it was believed that men were made in God's image and women in men's image, or at least partly in man's image. Viewing Eve and subsequently all women through the shadows of the Fall, women were understood to be inferior, less adequate than men. Characteristics traditionally viewed as feminine were viewed negatively. Yet here in Scripture we see that both male and female are made in the image and likeness of God. Both men and women carry God's nature and characteristics; both reflect something of what God is like. When we think of being made in God's or man's image, our thoughts often drift to a reflection in a mirror, forgetting that mirrors weren't used in Eden! Scholars note that the word "image" is also translated "imprint." When he made us, he left his mark on us, his imprint seared deeply through our being—so much so that it's only in oneness with him that we are complete, that we realize the fullness of our design. Only in relationship with him can the blueprint make sense.

This is good news for us women; our identity is formed by our Creator, our heavenly Father. We are made in his image, his likeness—it's with him that we find the basis of our true identity. He defines us and gives both men and women a purpose on earth. Women are not an afterthought in God's mind; we are a central part of his creative plan for the world!

What are the implications of being made in God's image and likeness? Think of those dreams and passions, for your office and work colleagues, your homes, your community, and your town or city. Did God sear his passion and dreams on your heart? Or that relational side, that passion for relationships, to nurture and cherish people? Perhaps you are reflecting back something of your Father's likeness? That strength you have, that visionary side, the initiator within you—could you believe that those parts of your character in their purest form reflect something of the Father's likeness too?

PEOPLE WITH A PURPOSE

God blessed them and said to them, "Be fruitful and increase in number;
fill the earth and subdue it. Rule over the fish in the sea and the birds
in the sky and over every living creature that moves on the ground."

Then God said, "I give you every seed-bearing plant on the
face of the whole earth and every tree that has fruit
with seed in it. They will be yours for food.

And to all the beasts of the earth and all the birds in the sky and all

the creatures that move on the ground—everything that has the breath
of life in it—I give every green plant for food. And it was so.

God saw all that he had made, and it was very good.

Genesis 1:28-31 tniv

In his original plan, God commissions humanity in partnership. Not only are we created to be with God, to walk intimately with him, sharing his image and likeness, humanity is given a job to do as his earthly representatives. The Bible tells us that, yes, women are designed for intimate relationship, but we're also designed for responsibility.

Adam and Eve are called to the task and awesome opportunity of living productive lives as part of God's new creation:

• They are called to be fruitful, to reproduce to fill the earth.

• They are called to subdue the earth and rule over it.

Still, these verses don't carve up the roles, or suggest a hierarchy in the tasks given; it's a joint commission to both men and women to multiply and to rule.

What could it mean if we fully grasped our call, our design for both relationship and responsibility? We know that to be fruitful, to multiply, can't exclusively refer to having children. Otherwise what would that mean for women with no children? And what would that say to our young adult women or teenagers passionate to be deployed for the kingdom's cause? If we fully grasped our call, would we hear echoes of Eden in the Great Commission—the call to make disciples, as we go through daily life, investing in others every single thing that the Lord has invested in us? Perhaps we would tell people about Jesus, share our faith—and see new birth. Perhaps we would disciple people, pour our lives into them. Perhaps we would hear echoes of Jesus' words at his ascension, telling his disciples that in the power of his Spirit they would be witnesses, in the city, in the regions, across cultures, across the world. And we'd realize that those words included us—no matter what walk of life we came from—because, regardless of gender, we are designed for this. Perhaps then we would we see ourselves as God's representatives in our communities and places of work, living out his kingdom rule in words, works and wonders that we see in the life of Jesus. We need to understand and embrace that a call to godly influence isn't automatically masking worldly ambition or broken secular values, but is intrinsic to our God-given design. Some of us may gravitate more naturally to the relational side, the intimacy with God. Others may gravitate more easily to the task, the kingdom responsibility we've been given. We've been designed and called to both.

LOST IN TRANSLATION

*The LORD God said, "It is not good for the man to
be alone. I will make a helper suitable for him."*

GENESIS 2:18

There are two creation accounts in Genesis. These words are taken from the second account, giving us a more detailed understanding of the woman we meet briefly in the first chapter.

This verse evokes a range of emotions, from satisfaction to disillusionment to sheer frustration and anger. Some women step back from the Bible at this point, writing it off as an archaic text and therefore irrelevant. Some go further, seeing this verse as one example of where the Bible—and therefore God—is misogynistic and has nothing positive to say about women, and considering the Bible as a religious tool for their oppression.

Others have raised the concern that it suggests that a woman is incomplete and has nothing to contribute to society unless she is married. What happens if you are single, divorced, widowed? Does a woman have no worth or value outside of her marital status? It raises the issues of what this means for the women with high-power careers, with major influence in their companies, of the entrepreneurial businesswomen. Should they expect or desire to rise to the top of their profession if they are "helpers"? Others just find it a bit confusing in light of the Scriptures themselves, wondering how women like Deborah, Phoebe and Lydia were helpers in the contemporary sense of the word.

There are certain passages in Scripture that are like the reference section in a library; they require more time and perhaps some help in navigating! If ever there was a word lost in translation, it is the word "helper." It's a word that requires deeper study to grasp the depth of its meaning (not to find a meaning that we feel comfortable with, just simply to understand what it means). A closer look at the word "helper" in Old Testament Hebrew illuminates what has been at first glance an alienating verse for many men and women.

Chambers Dictionary defines a helper thus:

noun
someone who helps; an assistant; an assistant minister (*archaic*)

And *Roget's Thesaurus* lists the following as synonyms for "helper":

help, assistant, aider, lieutenant, henchman, aide, right-hand man *or* woman, man Friday, girl Friday, amanuensis

The Hebrew word translated "helper," or in older translations of the Bible "helpmeet," is the word *ezer* (think "razor"). There are over a hundred references of the root of this word in the Old Testament, and about twenty-one references that use the identical word. Incredibly, the vast majority of times that this word appears are in reference to God, often when he is delivering his people. The woman is an *ezer*, and so is God. We're made in his image, and his potential resides in us!

Ezer is a powerful word. Scholar R. David Freeman observes that it is a combination of two words, one meaning "to rescue," "to save," the other meaning "to be strong."[2] Dr. Walter Kaiser, theologian and author, notes that *ezer* appears in the Old Testament often in parallel with words denoting strength or power.[3]

The word *ezer* does not mean that a woman should never be an assistant, an ally, a supporter. There is nothing pejorative about a man or a woman helping someone, or being called by the Lord to fulfill that role! It's always a privilege to serve him as we serve others. But it is also crucial that we understand that in the biblical definition of "helper" the *ezer* can also fulfill a different role. It seems that *ezer* has more to do with what helping looks like, because it doesn't seem to suggest anything about hierarchy. In some instances, *ezer* is a word with military connotations; the *ezer* is also a warrior. In this context, help comes from one who has the power and strength to provide it. *Ezer* is a verb as well as a noun, meaning "to defend, protect, surround and cherish."[4] The *ezer* is an amazing mix of strength, power, proactivity and vulnerability.

> Q. You may not like the idea of being a helper, but how do you feel about being an *ezer*?

A SUITABLE WOMAN WITH A SUITABLE LIFE

The LORD God said, "It is not good for the man to
be alone. I will make a helper suitable for him."

GENESIS 2:18

Kenegedu, often translated "suitable" or "fit" in this verse, appears only once in the Bible. Yet certain scholars argue that translations such as "suitable," "fit" or "appropriate" don't quite capture the word's breadth and intensity. The word comes from *neged*, which means "opposite" or "parallel to," so sometimes the phrase here is often translated "corresponding to." However, in later Hebrew the root *keneged* means "equal."

Sometimes in translation it has been merged with "helper," resulting in the translation "helpmeet" or "helpmate." But Kaiser argues against this, explaining that the Old English *meet*, meaning "suitable," slipped into a new English word, *mate*.[5]

Lost in translation indeed! Kaiser concludes that God's intention was for woman to be a "power" or strength, who would in every respect "correspond to" the man—that is, be "his equal." Freeman draws the same conclusion, stating "when God concluded that he would create another creature so that man would not be alone, he decided to make 'a power equal to him,' someone whose strength was equal to man's."[6]

So what does our heavenly Father say when he calls woman *ezer kenegedu*? He says that Eve, the blueprint, is not walking a few steps behind, subordinate by definition, lesser in some way. She is intended to be "a power equal to him." That's how he sees us. The implications are massive: yes, for marriage, but actually for every relationship between a man and a woman—at home, church, in the community, at work. As James writes, "The man and the woman were God's A team—his first string of all-stars called to fulfill his ambitious mandate."[7] God wanted more than schisms—in his design we'd work together in response to his commission.

> Q. **What difference does it make to realize that God sees you this way? How does it affect your relationship with him?**
>
> **How does it affect your call to influence the world around you?**

EVERYDAY *EZERS*

When God looked down on earth and made women, he was thinking of *ezer*s. And you don't have to look too far in everyday life to see them. They are the women who are not waiting for life to happen, but are living productive lives where they are. They are strong helpers, and for some that is a supportive role, an assistant. But for others it is a role of prominent influence. Both are *ezers*. We see the *ezer* in the mother who nurtures her children, in the woman in the neighborhood who lobbies the council to get better lighting to keep the streets safe for the community. She's the university student who campaigns against injustice, the prayer warrior who does battle in prayer for local schools. She is the loving wife who supports her husband in his career and is the bedrock of her family. She's the teacher, the doctor, the teenager; she's the missionary and she's the church leader.

We see the strength and power of the *ezer* expressed in everyday ordinary life. It's in the thirty-five years (!) of monthly menstrual cycles, in the labor pains and the screams and pushes of childbirth, in embracing the changes of menopause. But we know strength is not just a physical thing. The *ezer* is also the bridesmaid who smiles with grace and joy at her best friend's wedding, quietly surrendering her own personal longings for a husband. She's the woman who lovingly embraces her godchild while contending with the heartache of prolonged infertility. The *ezer* is that woman with the hot flashes imposing themselves on her body who still laughs at the days to come. *Ezers* emerge from an operating room, scarred, even maimed in battle, and they rest, convalesce, then in time get up and get back to work. *Ezers* are fighters—for their friends, their families, their communities, their churches, their nations. But their strength doesn't cost them their womanhood, their femininity. They've learned that their strength is feminine. You see, it's part of their God-given design.

Is there a piece of your identity that needs slotting back into place? A piece you never knew was missing? What does it mean to know that God calls you to both relationship and responsibility? Can you finally see yourself in Eve now, in her gait and her stride?

What does it mean for your understanding of leadership, of being an influential woman—that he names you *ezer kenegedu*? That *this* is how your heavenly Father made you, that this is your God-given design, and so your true potential?

Women are daughters of the King of all kings, but why would we want to play princesses waiting to be rescued when we can be *ezers*? We bear the image of the King, but we're here on earth for more than just to look attractive. Keep your tiara for another play date. We're commissioned alongside our brothers to see the kingdom come on earth, to see lives changed, to rebuild society.

Hamlet got it wrong when he said, "Frailty, thy name is woman." Woman, thy name is *ezer*.

We also need to meet some of the women in the Bible who responded to God's call in a range of ways. We need to look at their lives and stay awhile—perhaps we'll identify with them, see something of ourselves, in their gait, their stride. And we need to see how women through history have lived out their calling before God— maybe the timbre of their voices will resonate with our own, the cadence of their calling connect with ours. And perhaps we will not feel that we are so isolated, the only ones doing it. Perhaps we will not feel frustrated at having no one to learn from. Instead, we may discover that we are—that we've always been—part of a tribe of everyday people, living simply to love and serve the King.

Reflections on Leadership

Graham Cray, former Bishop of Maidstone, England:

Trust your instincts to lead—don't be pressured by existing (often male) ways of working.

Root yourself in Scripture—you cannot know it too much.

Remember that authority is not the same as control. Authority leaves space for and encourages the work of God through others that is beyond your own gifting.

Gareth Robinson, worship leader and church leader:

Be yourself (you're a woman, not a man!). The female perspective is a gift to the Church.

I'm always encouraged by female worship leaders who change the pitch of songs so they can lead them by singing confidently in their range. Many songs written by men are hard for women to sing; changing the pitch is an outward expression of female leaders being true to who they are.

The Cloud of Witnesses

Therefore, since we are surrounded by such a great cloud of witnesses,
let us throw off everything that hinders and the sin that so easily entangles,
and let us run with perseverance the race marked out for us.

HEBREWS 12:1

IF, IN OUR EYES, EVE HAS BECOME the broken picture of what it meant to be an *ezer*, it begs the question of what an *ezer* looks like when she walks with God, living in the fullness of her identity. What would we see, what would we discover? In this chapter we're going to explore the family tree of the people of God. We'll look at the lives of a few women in the Bible, both the New and Old Testaments. Who were they, how did they live, and what could that mean for us? Perhaps we'll understand our calling as we reflect on theirs. Maybe we'll resonate with their voices, identify with their stride, and see something of our lives in theirs. Even though they are all *ezers*, we find incredible diversity among the women of the Bible. But we're looking for a family resemblance, a redemptive picture of what an *ezer* could be. These women's lives reawaken us and reconnect us to our God-given heritage.

OLD TESTAMENT WOMEN

Few today contest the fact that women appear in a variety of ministry roles in the Old Testament. The key questions are,

Were these *leadership* roles? Did the community of faith affirm women in such positions? The biblical record yields a yes on both accounts.[1]

When God spoke through the prophet Micah to remind them of his faithfulness to them in times past, he said, "I brought you up out of Egypt and redeemed you from the land of slavery. I sent Moses to lead you, also Aaron and Miriam" (Micah 6:4).

Broken by the curse of slavery, the Israelites had cried out to God for generations for liberation from the oppression of the Egyptians. The brutality began when Pharaoh became afraid of the sheer number of Israelites in the land. He ordered that every newborn Israelite boy should be killed immediately. When Moses was born, his mother knew it was merely a question of time. So she placed him in a basket on the Nile, hopeful and prayerful that her son would escape. When Pharaoh's daughter found Moses, a young woman stood watching and waiting. Bravely she approached Pharaoh's daughter and arranged for her baby brother to be nursed by their mother. Years later she stood with her brother again, this time to lead God's people out of Egypt into their freedom. The passage above from Micah teaches us that, many generations after the exodus, Miriam is clearly seen as a key leader among God's people at this definitive stage of Israel's history. She is also described as a prophetess—one who communicates God's heart, perspective and counsel on a situation and (to use Paul's definition in 1 Corinthians 14:3) comforts, encourages and strengthens the community. In addition, Miriam is a worship leader, leading God's people with Moses in music and dance after the Egyptian armies are finally defeated in the Red Sea (Exodus 15).

The era of the judges was a turbulent one as God's people lived a cyclical pattern: disobedience to God, foreign invasion, crying out to God in distress, and finally God raising up a leader to bring deliverance. One of those leaders was a woman called Deborah.

> In the days of Shamgar son of Anath,
>> in the days of Jael, the highways were abandoned;
>> travelers took to winding paths.
> Villagers in Israel would not fight;
>> they held back until I, Deborah, arose,
>> until I arose, a mother in Israel. (Judges 5:6-7 TNIV)

Deborah was a prophetess, the wife of Lappidoth—a prophetess *and* Israel's leader/judge (Judges 4:4). As judge, Deborah was a highly respected figure in the community, and people sought her out to settle their disputes. Her leadership gift also served to unify the nation and lead them to war against the Canaanites, and gave Barak, the army leader, the military strategy to win the battle. Deborah was known as a *mother in Israel,* which Linda Belleville describes as an honor acknowledging her contribution to the country and her people on a national scale.[2] As a political and spiritual leader and the prophetic voice God's people needed, Deborah rebuilt the nation and restored it to community. And her success? The nation was at peace for a generation.

We often think that words like "ministry" and "calling" apply only to our churches. However, as we look at the men and women of the Bible, our heroes, we find that many of them served in "secular" roles. Nonetheless, they served and led while moving in God's grace, wisdom and power. Those of us who have influential roles the workplace—offices, departments, management, politics, education, health and media—must take note of the degree of influence God has given us. Have we fully engaged with our jobs as our calling?

Josiah was the first God-fearing king for many years. His father and grandfather walked away from God, worshiping idols, shedding innocent blood, leading their nation astray. Josiah, however, tore down the idolatrous worship sites and sought to restore God's temple. There, Hilkiah the priest found the long-neglected Book of the Law. When it was read aloud, Josiah was devastated, aware that God's people had rejected God's way of life and ignored the contents of this book. He needed to know what to do next, how to respond. He needed God's perspective on this tragedy. So he sent out Hilkiah and a delegation to establish the next step. Bypassing the priests, the delegation sought out a woman called Huldah.

> Go and inquire of the LORD for me and for the people and for
> all Judah about what is written in this book that has been found.
> . . . Hilkiah the priest, Ahikam, Acbor, Shaphan and Asaiah
> went to speak to the prophetess Huldah. (2 Kings 22:13-14)

For Huldah to have such a key voice in the country, without a position among the king's advisers, indicates the measure of her influence. Huldah shared a prophetic word which the king and his advisers responded to immediately, and a spiritual reformation happened.

This is by no means an exhaustive list. We know that Sarah, Ruth, Hannah and Esther were influential in a range of ways, and we'll meet them in later chapters. But for now it's interesting to note that in Old Testament times we see women with powerful influential roles in their faithful service to God.

WOMEN IN THE TIME OF JESUS

In an essay on the role of the women in society, novelist Dorothy L. Sayers (who graduated with first-class honors from Oxford before women were awarded degrees there, and was later a contemporary of C. S. Lewis) reflected on Jesus' relationship with women:

> Perhaps it is no wonder that the women were first at the Cradle
> and last at the Cross. They had never known a man like this
> Man—there never has been such another. A prophet and

teacher who never nagged at them, never flattered or coaxed or patronised; who never made arch jokes about them, never treated them either as "The women, God help us!" or "The ladies, God bless them!"; who rebuked without querulousness and praised without condescension; who took their questions and arguments seriously; who never mapped out their sphere for them, never urged them to be feminine or jeered at them for being female; who had no axe to grind or no uneasy male dignity to defend; who took them as he found them and was completely unself-conscious. There is no act, no sermon, no parable in the whole Gospel that borrows its pungency from female perversity; nobody could possibly guess from the words and deeds of Jesus that there was anything "funny" about women's nature.[3]

Who were the women in Jesus' life?

Mary, first at the cradle. In some ways Mary is easily forgotten because she is so obvious. But the young betrothed woman was integral to the turning point of human history for all time. It's amazing to think that Mary would have been in her teens when she received the news from Gabriel that she would carry the Messiah. It's even more significant when we realize that this call had the potential to ruin her standing in the community, break her engagement and destroy her family. Still, any pain and confusion she experienced here would only be the tip of the sword that would pierce her own heart and soul in the years to come. Nonetheless, her song of praise reflecting Hannah's song in 1 Samuel suggests a depth and a maturity in her relationship with God.

Mary nurtures Jesus as any good mother would, but from time to time is confronted with the reality that she has to let him go as he becomes all that he is meant to be. And the letting go will take her all the way to the sheer agony of the cross, where she watches helplessly as her firstborn son is crucified. The sword has pierced her soul and torn her in two. Yet this is not the end of Mary's story. We find a postscript in Acts 1:14, where we see Mary as part of the new church community, praying and waiting to receive the promised Holy Spirit. Traditions suggest she ultimately ended up in Ephesus with John, serving the church there.

We have so much to learn from Mary at every stage of her life. There's the teenager who embraces her unique calling with a song of praise in the face of staggering cost. There's the fretting mother as Jesus grows older, attempting to interfere and fix things. There's the cross, where the dream dies. Then finally Mary's new life and role in the early church.

Mary's example shows us that life can often lead us into uncharted territory.

> Q. Are we willing to accept the calling (and the limitations) that comes with every season of our lives? Could we surrender to God when we don't understand, or will we insist on interfering and fixing God's plan?
>
> Are we prepared for the ongoing cost of our God-given influence—even a pierced soul? What would that look like in our lives?
>
> And when our dreams die, can we rise again and embrace God's call on us for a new era?

The women in Jesus' life, death and resurrection. The Gospels tell many stories of Jesus' interaction with women. From his humble beginnings there are women who recognize and proclaim his significance. Alongside Mary, we see Elizabeth proclaim his lordship (Luke 1:41-45). When Jesus is taken to the temple to be presented to the Lord, as was customary for all firstborn, the young family meet Simeon, who prophesies over the family, and then they meet Anna. Anna, a prophetess, speaks about Jesus to everyone in the temple waiting for the redemption of Jerusalem (Luke 2:38). In Jesus' dealings with women, he repeatedly challenges the assumptions and cultural blind spots of the day. Jesus heals a number of women—Peter's mother-in-law (Luke 4:38-39), Jairus's daughter, but also the woman who had hemorrhaged for twelve years and was considered unclean (Luke 8:40-56). He saved the life of the woman caught in the act of adultery (John 8). And his conversation with a Samaritan woman with a history of broken relationships transforms her into the evangelist for her community (John 4).

The Gospels reveal that a number of women played influential roles in ministry alongside Jesus. When Jesus traveled, it's often assumed that it was only the Twelve who traveled with him. However, Luke introduces us to members of the wider missionary team.

> The Twelve were with him, and also some women who had been cured of evil spirits and diseases: Mary (called Magdalene) from whom seven demons had come out; Joanna the wife of Cuza, the manager of Herod's household; Susanna; and many others. These women were helping to support them out of their own means. (Luke 8:1-3)

These women played a fundamental role as they invested their money and resources into God's mission. Scholars reflect that they were probably wealthy upper-class women who had been healed and transformed by Jesus' ministry. But the women were more than sponsors; they were committed to Jesus and the cause, right to the end. Scholars note that "the verb used to designate their following of Jesus is *akoloutheo* (or its compounds), a term which occurs over seventy-five times in the Gospels and normally means following Jesus in the sense of being a disciple."[4]

Some people contend that if Jesus really believed in women leaders, why didn't he pick one to be one of the twelve disciples, his most intimate group? However, it's not only women who are not a part of the Twelve: there are no Gentiles, nor do we see a range of ethnicities. We've not denied these groups leadership opportunities as a result! It is radical enough that in an era where the place of women was largely limited to domestic roles, marriage and motherhood, where women were not always affirmed, that Jesus himself both affirmed women and carved out a wider role for them. Scholar Craig Evans states that "one of the astonishing features in Jesus' ministry was the presence of women disciples and associates among his followers. Women accompanying Jesus and his disciples would have been completely contrary to Jewish customs."[5]

In spite of all cultural limitations, women did play an incredible role in the final stages of Jesus' ministry on earth. When all the Twelve but John had deserted Jesus, the women were at the cross. On that first Easter Sunday, it was the women who were the first to see the empty tomb. It was the women who were visited by angels with the news of the resurrection. Finally, it is to one of the women, Mary Magdalene, that Jesus appears, and she is the one instructed to share the news with the disciples. We're so used to reading these stories that we may not understand how significant this is. At that time a women's testimony was not recognized in a court of law. Yet Jesus entrusted the most important news in human history to a woman and sent her to share it. As a result, early Christian writings described her as an apostle to the apostles. "Jesus entrusted the women with vital information about himself that the men needed to know. His apostles could not understand, much less preach or write about, the core events of Christianity—Jesus' birth, death, burial and resurrection—without learning from the women."[6] That's how significant the women were in the Gospels. What would we share without the proclamation of what they witnessed?

WOMEN IN THE NEW TESTAMENT

Jesus' respect for and inclusion of women as disciples and proclaimers provided the foundation for the positive place of women in the earliest churches and their ministry.[7]

The story of influential women continues throughout the New Testament as the message of the gospel continues to spread throughout the known world.

Lydia—the gateway to Europe. Philippi was a Roman colony and an important city in Macedonia, seen as the gate to Europe for trade and commerce, but when it came to the gospel moving into Europe it was a woman named Lydia who was the gateway. Paul and the team made their way to Macedonia, convinced that they needed to share the gospel after Paul had had a vision of a Macedonian man pleading, "Come over to Macedonia and help us" (Acts 16:9). Because there was no synagogue, the team went to the river, known to be a place of prayer.

Lydia was a dealer in expensive purple cloth, a successful businesswoman with a household that included servants. But for all her success, there was an emptiness that led her to the river's edge. There she met Paul and heard the gospel for the first time, becoming the first convert in Europe. So Lydia (and members of her household) was baptized. But she doesn't stop there. Lydia is bold and persuades the apostolic team to make her home their base, and when they leave, Lydia's home becomes the first home of the Philippian church (Acts 16:40).

Pioneering women. "Apostle" comes from the Greek word *apostolos*, meaning "sent ones," "sent forth with orders," "a delegate."

> Apostles are visionary and pioneering, always pushing into new territory. They like to establish new churches or ministries. They come up with new innovative means to do kingdom work.[8]

The New Testament introduces us to a number of apostolic women. Priscilla, also known as Prisca, was married to Aquila, a Jew from Pontus. Paul commends Priscilla and Aquila as his coworkers, describing how they risked their lives for him and highlighting their influence within the wider church.[9] Paul worked alongside them as tentmakers in Corinth and they journeyed with him to Ephesus (a key training center for the New Testament church), establishing the church there as Paul continued to travel. One of their roles included discipling and teaching the apostle Apollos. They also had a church that met in their home (1 Corinthians 16:19). It's interesting to note that, where Priscilla and Aquila appear in the New Testament, in six places, when referring to the tent-making business and their house, Aquila's name appears first. When referring to ministry, including the discipling of Apollos, Priscilla's name is first. It was common in their culture for the man's name to appear first when referring to a couple (as is still the case today), denoting his prominence. Is this significant? John Chrysostom, a church father writing in the fourth century A.D., thought so.

> For he did not say "Greet Aquila and Priscilla," but "Priscilla and Aquila." He does not do this without a reason, but he seems to me to acknowledge a greater godliness for her than her husband.[10]

Tertullian, another early church father, also acknowledged Priscilla's role in communicating the gospel. But perhaps most significant is that both Chrysostom and Tertullian are known for making negative statements about women generally (Tertullian described women as "the devil's gateway"), yet openly acknowledge Priscilla's significance as a leader in the New Testament. Many theologians believe Priscilla was actually the more prominent ministry leader of the two, and some argue that Priscilla may actually have written the letter to the Hebrews.

Priscilla is a dynamic pioneer in the early church and a great example for influential women today.

In Romans 16:7 we meet another groundbreaker:

> Greet Andronicus and Junia, my fellow Jews who have been in prison with me. They are outstanding among the apostles, and they were in Christ before I was. (Romans 16:7 TNIV)

Junia is a woman whom Paul greets, highlights and commends as an apostle. Paul describes these relatives as people who have walked as Christians since before his own conversion. However, in the course of church history Junia became a hidden example of an apostolic woman when her name was lost in translation. In the earliest translations of the Bible, indeed for the first millennium, Junia was a woman. Church fathers such as Jerome, Origen and John Chrysostom refer to Junia as a woman, though none of them were particularly favorable toward women in general. Chrysostom comments on Romans 16:7:

> Greet Andronicus and Junia . . . who are outstanding among the apostles: To be an apostle is something great! But to be outstanding among the apostles—just think what a wonderful song of praise that is! They were outstanding on the basis of their works and virtuous actions. Indeed, how great the wisdom of this woman must have been that she was even deemed worthy of the title of apostle.[11]

However, in the thirteenth century, commentator Aegidus of Rome described her as a man, and the change began. Junia became Junias. Still, scholars note that "The masculine name Junias does not occur in any inscription, letterhead, piece of writing, epitaph, or literary work of the New Testament period. The feminine Junia, however, appears widely and frequently."[12]

Oh, the power of one little scribbled *s*! What has it cost us to lose Junia in translation? Generations of apostolic women who could have changed the world? Frustrated disenfranchised women who didn't know the Father's affirmation when he sent them out to a broken world as entrepreneurs or missionaries?

What does it cost us today?

Entrusted with the role of delivering Paul's letter to the Roman believers, Phoebe is described by Paul as a sister. But not only a sister;

Paul also describes her as *diakonos*, using the same word used to describe a male deacon.

> I commend to you our sister Phoebe, a servant [*diakonos*] of the church in Cenchrea. I ask you to receive her in the Lord in a way worthy of the saints and to give her any help she may need from you, for she has been a great help to many people, including me. (Romans 16:1-2)

The vast majority of times we see *diakonos* in the New Testament it refers to men and is translated "deacon" or "minister"; there is no feminine word for deacon in the Bible. Rodney Stark notes that "deacons were of considerable importance in the early church. They assisted at liturgical functions and administered the benevolent and charitable activities of the church."[13]

Phoebe is described as a great help to many people. But again we need to look closer to understand what that phrase actually means in its original context. The word here is *prostatis*, meaning "supervisor," "protector" or "patron."[14] Loren Cunningham and David Hamilton argue that "servant leader" is a better translation of *prostatis* than "great help," "because it describes a leader who champions the cause of others rather than pursuing self interest."[15] Is it inaccurate to call Phoebe a servant and a great help? No, these words are accurate, and every leader is called to serve and to help. But when we don't understand the full context and definition of these words in their own culture, Phoebe can sound like a helpful servant girl who kindly delivered a letter. We need to know that our forerunner did much more than that. Paul endorses his relationship with Phoebe and the significance of her role, clarifying her credentials within the Cenchrean church. Early church fathers such as Origen and Chrysostom considered Phoebe's role to be one of rank. Phoebe was a deacon in Cenchrea with influence and authority, a servant leader to many.

Women as oikos leaders. The household in New Testament times does not describe the form of nuclear family as we may understand it today. The word commonly translated "house" is *oikos*. In the first-century Greco-Roman world, the *oikos* included "not only the immediate family and relatives but also slaves, freedmen and freed-women, hired workers, even tenants and partners in trade or craft."[16] The *oikos* was both a social and an economic unit; to run a household was to effectively lead a community.

> Give my greetings to the brothers and sisters at Laodicea, and to Nympha and the church in her house. (Colossians 4:15 TNIV)

The early church did not have a permanent building, but mainly met in people's households, which served as an effective strategy for penetrating the community with the message of the gospel. Lydia led a household, as did Priscilla and Aquila, Chloe in Corinth and Nympha in Colossae, among others. A number of these small *oikos* leaders were women who were also very secure financially. Today many churches in the West are exploring how to be church and do church life in a way that reconnects with people who are interested in spirituality, but not in institutionalized church. There is a greater emphasis on missional living, on the life together as believers, and the *oikos* is making something of a comeback in the form of missional communities.

The examples of Nympha, Chloe and others speak to women who sense a call to build an authentic expression of Christian community in their neighborhood or among their network of relationships. Their lives intersect with those of their neighbors, their children's friends and parents, their work colleagues on a regular basis. There are many women who know that their home, not the church building, is a key place for "ministry." It happens around the kitchen table, through meals and conversation. Their home is balm for the worn and weary, for those who've not experienced God's love in a community. They seek to be the hands and feet and heart of Jesus in everyday living, influencing the world around them. The *oikos* was a powerful strategy for kingdom expansion in the New Testament, and as a model continues to be so today.

The final roll call. And there are more women, many more names. We discover Philip's four prophetic daughters, mentioned in the book of Acts. We meet Eunice and Lois, a mother and grandmother whose lives and influence bore fruit in one of the most significant leaders of the New Testament, Timothy. We meet Tryphaena and Tryphosa, Persis and Mary, whose ministry Paul describes using the same language as he did to describe the evangelism and ministry of his own colleagues—and himself.[17] We meet Euodia and Syntyche who, like Priscilla, are described by Paul as coworkers, a translation of *synergos*, which stems from a word meaning "to contend on the side of anyone," "to co-operate vigorously with a person."[18] Scholars Ben Witherington and Ann Witherington note that the word is a verb from athletic terminology used for gladiatorial matches and can mean "fought together side by side," concluding, "This hardly suggests a passive role in spreading the gospel."[19] These are more than names; they are women who served the Lord, amid challenge and persecution, in the midst of their everyday lives, and they influenced the world around them, they changed lives, they shaped communities. Like the men in the early church, they led the way and were pioneers in their time and through the ages. They were examples of what it means to live wholeheartedly in devotion to Christ and to respond to his calling.

Will we ignore the women we've discovered and the lives they've led?

WHAT ABOUT PAUL?

Did you notice that most of the New Testament women mentioned above worked with, and were commended by, the apostle Paul? Paul has often been called a misogynist, and his letters are quoted repeatedly suggesting that women should not take up positions of leadership. But we've seen that it is clear from the text that Paul did work with women, that he did endorse female leaders and the significant contribution that they made in advancing the gospel.

We don't need to ignore the more complex verses of Scripture, though some us would relish the chance to avoid them! We've been told that Paul calls for women to be silent in the churches, that women cannot teach men. Our hearts sank, and we walked away, wondering what this heavenly Father who loved us was thinking after all. Is the Bible good for women like us? Then we look at these women, these forerunners. Priscilla, Junia, Phoebe, Mary, Deborah . . . We absorb again who they were, what they actually did, the lives they actually led. It's now that we realize these few verses do not communicate or even summarize all that Paul says about women, let alone the rest of the Bible! We haven't taken cultural context into account, and translation difficulties. We haven't taken the women themselves into account. Years ago my pastor used to say that when it came to women in leadership, we have taken unclear or obscure verses and used them to reinterpret clear parts of the Bible. We have redefined Phoebe's role, and stress that she is a helpful servant rather than an influential deacon and servant leader because a silent woman couldn't possibly have such a large role. We change Junia's name because an apostle couldn't possibly be a woman. We say that Priscilla explaining the gospel to Apollos in Acts 18:26 is a completely different thing from teaching him because it seems to contradict 1 Timothy 2:12, where Paul seems opposed to women teaching men.

If, as my pastor recommended, we looked at the passages of Scripture that are clear, what could we see? We'd see Miriam and Deborah and Huldah and Esther. We'd see Mary and many of Jesus' female team. We'd see Phoebe, Lydia, Priscilla, Chloe, Junia—the list continues. We'd see the influential women God has raised up, whose lives positively affected both women and men.

And would we ignore those verses? No, we wouldn't.

As in all the congregations of the saints, women should remain silent in the churches. They are not allowed to speak, but must be in submission, as the Law says. If they want to inquire about something, they should ask their own husbands at home; for it is disgraceful for a woman to speak in the church. (1 Corinthians 14:33-35)

But we would make some observations and ask ourselves some questions. We'd acknowledge that Priscilla and Chloe were leaders of Corinthian church communities, and that Phoebe's church was based in Cenchrea, a suburb of greater metropolitan Corinth. Were they silent in the churches, and did Paul ever expect them to be? Paul had publicly worked with capable female leaders in Corinth. We'd also observe that the word translated "women" here is the same word as for "wives." Was Paul calling for silence among women in general, or a group of nattering wives with particularly loud voices? Furthermore, just a few chapters earlier, when talking about headship Paul speaks of the need for women to cover their heads when praying or prophesying in the context of the worship gathering (1 Corinthians 11:1-16). So clearly women were not expected to be silent all the time, because they prayed and prophesied in public. And while I am brushing past that topic of headship in 1 Corinthians 11, here is another concern for female leaders. It's interesting again to note the female leaders like Priscilla, who were a part of that faith community. Some have interpreted "headship"—the word *kephale*—to mean that a woman cannot lead or be more prominent than her husband. What does that mean for Priscilla, then? And what would that suggest about women like Deborah?

WHAT ABOUT *THIS* BIT?

A woman should learn in quietness and full submission. I do not permit a woman to teach or to have authority over a man; she must be silent.

1 Timothy 2:11-12

Let's make some observations. Timothy, the recipient of the letter quoted here, is based in Ephesus, overseeing the church there—a church that was started by a church-planting couple called Priscilla and Aquila. (Again, we see Priscilla playing a key role in the birth of this church community, a woman who taught Apollos and whom Paul endorsed.) Paul's ministry strengthened this church, and later Timothy becomes more involved. This was one of Paul's key churches. Mary the mother of Jesus is thought to have lived there, too, until she died. It was a church in the heart of the world; Ephesus was a thriving city, the fourth largest in the known world. Though not the official capital city, it was the greatest city, the one that everyone knew about. It was an academic city; it hosted annual sports events, had fabulous architecture, an excellent banking system and the most important harbor. It was seen as the gateway to Asia. Gods like the fertility goddess Artemis and Domitian were worshiped there, and because temple prostitution was part of the worship, it was home to thousands of such prostitutes. Promiscuity and occultism were rife, and a lot of money was made in the sex/religion industries.

This was a city where women held roles in public office and enjoyed more freedom than in other parts of the New Testament world. However, when it came to religion, women dominated the system. Theologians Richard Kroeger and Catherine Kroeger note that Artemis worship derived from an Amazonian tradition where women dominated and controlled the men.[20] Life was seen as cheap—babies would be found on the rubbish heap. It was also known as the highway for the martyrs because of the number of Christians taken through the city on their way to being executed in Rome.

One of Paul's major concerns in this letter is that heretical and worldly views are seeping into the life and teaching of the church. He commands that a woman must learn in silence and submission—it's worth nothing that this was exactly the same way male students were expected to learn. Was Paul making a complaint or calling for equality? Some scholars suggest that Paul addresses only one woman in this text about the content of her teaching, not women in general. Others stress that Paul writes largely about the nature of the teaching in this young church community, and note that the structure of Paul's sentence translated "I do not permit a woman to teach or have authority" in the original Greek text actually points more to *what* the woman is teaching, not whether she should be allowed to do so.

When Paul uses the word "authority" in other letters, he generally uses the word *exousia*. Here he uses *authentein*, a word not seen anywhere else in the New Testament and very rarely in ancient literature. As well as "to have authority over," it can also mean "to murder," "to domineer," "to be the master of." When we remember the cultural context and the values of Artemis worship (women dominating men), as well as all the other observations, could Paul be correcting a heresy in the context of church life, rather than making a general pronouncement about women? The Kroegers state that "the reader has a right to know that there is more than one plausible way to translate this verse."[21] These are just a few superficial observations and questions; much more has been written on these verses, and in far more detail, that you can look at to help you draw your own conclusion.

THE BIG QUESTION

Still, there are bigger observations to make and questions to ask when we look at influential women in the Bible. It's vital that we spend time investigating and exploring the Bible to see what women actually *did* do, what God called them to do and to be, both in the church and being sent from the church into the world around them. Theologian and author Scot McKnight suggests that, rather than limiting the discussion on women in leadership to the traditional debates, we should instead reframe our questions to look at what *women ministering* looked like in the Bible. Then we can ask whether we should do what the Bible clearly endorsed: "Do women *do* in your church what Miriam, Deborah, Huldah, Priscilla, Junia, and Phoebe did? Do they *do* what Mary did? Do they *do* what Jesus encouraged women to do?"[22] McKnight asks a sobering question, the implications of which might shatter our imaginative gridlock! These women had significant influence, leading churches, communities, movements and nations! Is our vision still too small, our understanding of our calling still too limited?

Perhaps we should just follow the example of humble, godly women in the Bible, women like Deborah, Lydia, Phoebe, Priscilla or Lois and Eunice, with lives fully surrendered to God, lives ready to embrace his call on his terms.

What would we do? How would we live? I believe we'd be both challenged and inspired to step into what God is calling us to in our day. And I believe we'll see his kingdom come in power in and through our lives.

Reflections on Leadership

Jon Shirley, worship leader and pastor:

Be brave and courageous, and if you must, humbly dissent.

In every age, when real prophetic change begins to emerge, it happens through the brave and few who will challenge the status quo, believing the status quo is not the greater truth.

Dissent is a powerful thing. When the revolutionary understands that it's really only through humility and powerlessness that truth can flow through them to bring effective difference, influence can then breed sustainable change. That's the wake-up call. The ones who only make noise will get popular, but they will be here today and gone tomorrow. The ones whose lives make real noise are those who understand the power of selfless influence. They will be the game-changers.

One thing I would love for young women [and young men] to understand is that influence is the way to create movement that moves in a new direction. What I mean by dissent is a life lived that challenges the status quo, yet in a way that will allow the host culture to embrace the change.

Roy Crowne, executive director of HOPE Together:

• *The gift of leadership is God-given rather than through manipulation or maneuver. There should be an acknowledgement that God opens opportunities to embrace and release those gifts of leadership.*

Calling

For I know the plans I have for you, declares the LORD.

JEREMIAH 29:11

Work is love made visible.

KAHLIL GIBRAN

SO WE UNDERSTAND THAT FROM the dawn of human history, men and women were fashioned to know God, but also given a commission from God. We've seen that women were designed as *ezer*s, a word far richer and more meaningful than the twenty-first-century definition of "helper" can possibly communicate. We've looked at some of the women of the Old and New Testaments and seen how God inhabited their lives and ignited their talents and used their circumstances, deploying them for the kingdom's cause. The writer to the Hebrews informs us that we stand before a great cloud of witnesses as we run our lap of life. It's our turn. So what are we supposed to do next?

How do we discover what our lives could look like?

CALLED TO LIVE LIKE JESUS

There are some big principles from the Bible that are integral to our calling and apply for everyone. As we've already discussed in the previous chapter, we're designed for both relationships and responsibility, so we can be confident that God has called our lives to reflect his intricate design. As Christians we've chosen to follow Jesus, to imitate him in every part of our lives. So when exploring our calling we can ask: what did Jesus do? A closer look at the life of Jesus highlights his three main priorities:[1]

- *A relationship with his Father.* This relationship was central to Jesus' life. It was a relationship he consistently invested in, through prayer, worship and a devotional life with God. Jesus was so dependent on his Father for his calling that he said he only did what he saw his Father doing (John 5:19).

- *Authentic relationships with other believers.* Jesus also prioritized his personal relationships, and lived in community with others. He gathered twelve disciples *to be with him* as well as to preach. But there were also other relationships with those who traveled with them (Mary, Susanna and Joanna, among others), and he invested time with other followers like Lazarus, Mary and Martha.

- *A relationship to the world around him, being good news expressed in evangelism and service.* Jesus shared the message of God's saving love in his words, both in conversations and in proclamations. He communicated God's love in the way he treated people, particularly as he reached out to the rejected and marginalized members of the community. He demonstrated God's power and love in his ministry and through miracles of healing and deliverance, and ultimately through his death and resurrection.

AND IF THE ANGEL GABRIEL DOESN'T TURN UP?

The Bible also shows that on occasion God gave specific directions about the context where his call would be expressed. Mary had an angel visitation. Moses had a burning bush and a call to go and set a nation free. Ezekiel fell face down after receiving an incredible vision and then was commissioned to a people group described as "stubborn and hard-hearted." Paul had a dream of a Macedonian man. So we also know that God brings clarity and direction to the general call. The major question is: *how*?

If there's no burning bush, no angel visitation, no dream or transcendent vision, how can we work out what God wants for our lives? Words such as "calling," "vocation," "destiny," "purpose" have an intimidating weightiness, a gravitas about them. They seem to be for pastors, missionaries off to dangerous places, or other Christian VIPs who will do "great things for God." Maybe only those people get the "calling."

It's not that we are without ideas; it's just that our ideas are not always God's ones! I can recall times in my life where I was absolutely certain that God had a given a clear word and plan. Once the vision was to be both Wonder Woman and a disco dancer (ages four to six). Then there was the call to be a multimillion-selling pop/soul legend and diva (ages seven to *way* too long). Or the one to marry particular individuals (we'll save that conversation for another book!).

Funnily enough, none of those things happened. And I was so sure about all of them! Now, with the benefit of hindsight, I see that for most of my life I have stumbled into relationships and opportunities that God has provided for me, uncertain or more often unaware of where he was in it all. Nothing was written in the sky; it's only in looking back that I've really begun to understand and see a pattern of how God has been working. As I've reflected on his hand on my journey, I've learned, and continue to learn, what calling might look like in practical, everyday terms.

If you are wondering what God may be calling you to do, consider the list of suggestions below. These are just a number of ways (often in tandem with each other) that God guides and gives us direction. There were so many things I felt I *should* be as a Christian woman that I often found myself doing things I wasn't gifted to do—and everyone suffered! There were so many voices and pressures, I needed some tools that would help me dig to find what God was doing in my life, what he'd always been doing. For me personally, looking at my personality type and fivefold ministry role (Ephesians 4:11-12, and see the section on gifts and roles later in this chapter) has been instrumental in my leadership development. It might be something completely different for you. The important thing is that we learn how to tune in to what God is saying and doing in our lives. Hopefully these suggestions will give you something to work with!

SPENDING TIME WITH GOD

This first one is really important!

Have you taken the time to pray about what God has for you, spent some time seeking God about your choices, decisions and plans? Perhaps taken a retreat that allows you some space to listen to God? It seems obvious, but I just know that I've spent time agonizing over a decision or a direction, and have forgotten to spend any time with God on it. When someone asks me if I've prayed, or if I've received any insights in my devotional times or Bible study, it's as though a light has dawned. . . . I've been so busy thinking, I've not done any seeking and listening! With that in mind, it makes sense to talk with him about these things, and to listen to and look out for his guidance and direction in our lives.

I very rarely have dreams that communicate anything more than the previous night's television, but for some of us God uses our dreams to communicate his plans. Or perhaps his direction arrives in a vision, a visual image that comes to mind or an internal impression that has simply stayed with you. You know you wouldn't have thought it up by yourself, and now the thought has lingered for such a long time that you wonder if it might mean anything. It's not a grand delusion or fantasy; it's something that reflects God's values and priorities in some way. A dream of serving your community in practical, tangible ways. A vision of reaching out to disaffected teenagers. An impression that you and your friends are called out of the suburbs and into long-forgotten urban areas to influence them for good. Could God be speaking to you?

WHAT'S IN YOUR HEART, WHAT'S ON YOUR MIND?

For others, clarity on calling comes from what is happening in their hearts. The biblical understanding of the heart is far more expansive than our definition of "heart" today. We might limit heart to our passions and emotions, whereas the biblical understanding of the heart includes our intellect, will, the core of our personality. So if I ask what God has put on your heart, it could mean a number of things! For some of us it will be through our emotions. There are situations in the world that anger us, others that make us cry. They are situations that make us want to get up and pray something, be something, do something. Could God be trying to get your attention? For others, God may flood our intellects and imagination. He'll ignite your mind with problem-solving systems and strategies for the world around you, inspire you with possibilities that only the imagination can grasp at this stage. In your opinion, it's just that— your opinion, ideas that no one else wants or needs to hear. Unless, of course, God has put them there. What thoughts are currently buzzing around your mind? What issues or situations have seared your thoughts and ignited your imagination? Could God be trying to direct your path?

ASK THE RIGHT QUESTIONS

"It's thirty years from now, and a dinner is being held in your honor. At some point someone stands up to propose a toast to you, but begins with a speech about you. What will they say you have done with your life?" My friend and colleague Steve asked me that question as I was trying to gain a sense of what God wanted me to do in a new season of life. Sometimes we can excavate some of the things the Lord has laid on our hearts by asking a few pertinent questions. The scenario Steve set for me helped me consider what really mattered to me, what I considered were things of eternal value. It helped me process what it meant to be faithful to God with the relationships and opportunities he'd given me over the years.

In his book *The Seven Habits of Highly Effective People*, Stephen Covey uses a similar tool, encouraging readers to consider the words spoken at their funeral by the people who knew them most at home, at work, at church. He challenges the reader to "begin with the end in mind": "How different our lives are when we really know what is deeply important to us, and, keeping the picture in mind, we manage ourselves each day to be and to do what really matters most."[2]

Other questions you could use as a tool to excavate what God has already laid on your heart:

- What would you do with your life if you knew you couldn't fail?

- What would you do with your life if you fully knew that God and the people around you gave you permission, encouragement and opportunity to lead?

I'm sure there are many other pertinent questions out there that could help you along your journey. Get together with some friends and write your own!

FRIENDS

Another great way to work out what God's doing in our lives and the adventures he's inviting us into is through our friends. Western culture seems to naturally default to individualism, including in our spirituality. Mike Breen notes that we've emphasized the quiet time and the pulpit as the primary areas where we expect to receive guidance and direction for our lives.[3] And calling seems like such a personal and private thing that we can forget the wonderful resource God has given us in trusted friends to help us on the journey of discovering his life for us. We see it in the Bible in David and Jonathan's friendship, and in the life of the early church. Mike concludes: "We need to be talking things through in families, with our colleagues, with friends, in our groups, at church. God could be trying to communicate something with us and we're missing it!"[4] Our friends often see our gifts and talents more clearly than we do. Where we would succumb to inadequacy or false humility, they can freely affirm and encourage us.

Like discovering your call, discovering the context for your call need not be an individualistic thing. Again, perhaps through a cultural or personal leaning toward individualism, we may overlook the fact that God's call for our lives has been communicated in the calling of our faith community. We may be called to get involved in someone else's initiative, serve someone else's vision, to connect with other people sharing the same heartbeat. Have you met people who are doing something you believe in and want to contribute to? Knowing that we are designed for both relationships and responsibility, it's no surprise that what God calls us to do can flow quite naturally from the people he's given us to do life with.

ATTENDING TO THE LIFE WE HAVE

Some of exploring the area of calling involves simply being intentional with the life we've been given. Perhaps some of the roles in our life feel too ordinary and normal to be attached to big words like "calling." But just because it's obvious doesn't mean it's not from God. Our heroes from Scripture, both men and women, were ordinary people too. They were married, they were single, they were parents and grandparents. They had a range of jobs in which they served the Lord full time, because their lives *were* their ministries. Remember Lydia, the businesswoman who happened to have a house church. Priscilla and Aquila were tentmakers who happened to be an incredible apostolic team. Daniel, Shadrach, Meshach and Abednego were in government with increasing influence and opportunity, while serving in an alien and often hostile environment. Other leaders were shepherds or fishermen. And God did incredible history-making things with them and through them in the contexts of their jobs, their families, their awful histories and their present circumstances. Their lives, anonymous (at the time at least, for many of them) and God-infused, were their calling. Yet so often we consider that calling and vocation apply only to a person called into "full-time Christian ministry," serving in the church or on the mission field.

What would it look like if we threw away such a limited worldview and embraced the call to a God-infused life? If we explored the implications of the call or vocation of being a friend, wife, mother, child? Or being a member of that team at work? Would we live differently? Pray differently, act differently? Would it redefine our use of time, money and effort? When relationships were strained, would we be more likely to see whether reconciliation was possible? What if we attended to our jobs as though they were our God-given vocation? Or engaged with our churches as if they were the community the Lord himself had given us? Would we see fresh potential? Could God use us there?

(SUPER)NATURAL TALENT

Sometimes part of the excavation process is exploring, discovering and even rediscovering gifts and talents. What do you enjoy? What are you good at doing? Some of these things will already be apparent—you may love gathering groups of people together, or host great parties; you may be a great listener or love to be creative. Maybe you're the one always called on to organize or lead committees. Often, we don't consider these gifts; they are things that just come naturally to us, just what we do. Let's remember, though, that even the things that come naturally to us come from him, and it's worth taking another look at some of the gifts and talents we think are "just the way we are." There are tools often found in the sphere of leadership development and training that can contribute great insights into some of our "natural" gifts. Personality assessments such as the Myers-Briggs Type Indicator or StrengthsFinder may show you something about how God's wired you that you might not have seen or explored before.

GIFTS AND ROLES

The New Testament teaches us that God in his grace and power has poured out gifts and roles among his people. In Romans 12, Paul encourages the church community to release and use their gifts:

> If it is encouraging, let him encourage; if it is contributing to the needs of others, let him give generously; if it is leadership, let him govern diligently; if it is showing mercy, let him do it cheerfully. (Romans 12:8)

In 1 Corinthians 12, Paul gives examples of the gifts of the Spirit that are poured out when the people are gathered together. They include gifts of prophecy, wisdom, healings and signs and wonders. In Jesus we see that these gifts were not limited to the church services, but were demonstrations of the love of God when people in the community encountered Jesus and his disciples. People are healed, lives liberated from demonic oppression. The outcasts are shown mercy, the guilty set free. Signs and wonders point to an eternal kingdom, and a King of kings.

What gifts of the Spirit do you see at work in and through your life? Are there things that you do, ways that you serve, where you are especially aware of his power and strength at work?

In Ephesians 4, a more general letter to churches in a region, Paul writes of five roles or functions that we can expect to see alive and well among the body of Christ:

> It was he who gave some to be apostles, some to be prophets, some to be evangelists, and some to be pastors and teachers, to prepare God's people for works of service, so that the body of Christ may be built up until we all reach unity in the faith and in the knowledge of the Son of God and become mature, attaining to the whole measure of the fullness of Christ. (Ephesians 4:11-13)

We've come to see these roles as job titles for Christian leaders within the church. Again, we remember that the life and fabric of the early church were very different from our own, gathering in people's homes, built around households, resourcing one another, connecting with nonbelievers in a far more incarnational way. These roles reach beyond the church's walls.

The apostles are the sent ones, the pioneers, with visions and strategies for new ideas. They are the innovators. They could be planting new churches and ministries or missionary endeavors, or in the workplace as the natural entrepreneurs and explorers. In the New Testament we know that Paul was an apostle, among many others including Junia, the woman we learned of in the previous chapter.

The prophetic types listen to God and articulate his perspective, either about the future or into a present-day situation. God has wired them to be especially perceptive—they often see things that others just don't see, and have a sense of what God is up to. They're often the creative people, the musicians, artists, poets, communicating something beyond the everyday world. Agabus is another prophet we meet in Acts, as well as Philip's prophetic daughters.

The teachers love the truth and making sure that people grasp it. In the church they *love* the Bible and studying and learning, and inspire others to do the same. In the workplace they'll be coaching, teaching, training and developing. Apollos was clearly a significant teacher in the New Testament.

Evangelists share good news and are good news! In the church the evangelists are often frustrated because there are not enough non-Christians around, and as far as they are concerned the church needs to get out there more! They naturally end up in conversations with people about the good news, because like a sales rep or PR person they're passionate about what they believe in. Philip and Steven were evangelists. And it could certainly be argued that the Samaritan woman in John 4:29, who called out after her encounter with Jesus, "Come, see a man who told me everything I ever did. Could this be the Christ?" was an evangelist too.

Pastors care for, nurture and protect others; they value hospitality and time with people. They're great listeners. The pastor *in* the church is not limited to the pastor *of* the church. There are loads of professions with a pastoral emphasis—counselors, nurses and the caring professions. Who were the pastoral types in the Bible? The *oikos* leaders, perhaps: people like Barnabas, who was known as the Son of Encouragement.

What about you? Do you see yourself operating in any of these roles?

This brief introduction to the roles in Ephesians 4 only gives a basic framework. It's just to get you to start thinking about how the Lord has wired you. You'll see all of these roles in your life at some point; we're not one-dimensional characters who can be simply labeled! Nor is it an excuse to avoid witnessing by saying "I'm not an evangelist," or caring for others because "I'm not a pastor." Jesus exemplified all of these roles in his life and ministry, and it's him we imitate. However, when you reflect upon your life, you may see one of these functions is more visible, more often, than others. It's as though you just keep coming back to it, as though it's your place in his body. When our then-church-leader Mike Breen unpacked Ephesians 4 with our church in Sheffield, it released hundreds of men and women to rediscover who God had designed them to be and understand what that could look like practically. It was incredibly empowering.[5]

Ask other leaders how their calling unfolded and what advice they have for you. Someone else's experience and perspective can inform your own and help you understand God's workings in your own life. With that in mind, I'll leave the final thoughts of this chapter in the hands of some fantastic leaders sharing what they have learned about calling.

Reflections on Calling

Anne Maclaurin, senior vicar at St. Barnabas, Cambridge:

If somebody comes to me saying I've burnt out my last vision, I'm moving on from a vision or I have no idea what my vision is, I say— start by serving. Simply serve. You'll find that you never stop serving; serving is a fundamental part of leadership. Too often people say, "I don't have a vision so I'm not going to do anything." My advice is start serving somewhere, get engaged in what someone else is doing, and see where that leads you.

Jeanette Baker, executive pastor in Colorado:

Calling is a process. Calling forms out of many small experiences, typically over several seasons of your life. Be patient with the process of discovering your calling. Make sure it aligns with what is true of you in passions, spiritual gifts and strengths. You may need to grow in these areas; the goal is to discern that your calling is definitely in your wheelhouse. It somehow should relate to what people tell you you are good at and experiences that you want to keep doing.

Once you are sure of this, do not make apologies for your initiative in pursuing your calling. It is good to have clarity of soul and to be confident in pursuing it. What is not good is to declare your calling to everyone: that feels more like self-promotion to people and they distrust it, especially those who are in leadership above you. Speak from a place of humility. *Share what you feel drawn to and passionate about. Go to those who have led you in the past or have known you through seasons of your life and ask for their input. When you have clarity about next steps in your calling, seek opportunity to take small steps, put into practice the self-discipline and spiritual disciplines that will be required. Seek books, a mentor and other learning opportunities you will need to experience, grow and one day become a master in that area. Be willing to put in the hours and work required to more fully understand, hone the skills and clarify your calling.*

Emma Andrews, young professional, wife and mother:

Someone once talked about discipleship and leadership in terms of gathering or observing people who want to learn from you or just simply spend time with you. . . . It has really helped me understand the way I relate to people and how I am a leader. It obviously isn't the definitive definition, but I found it a good place to start.

I have felt called for a long time to the workplace, and my immediate thought was that to "lead" in the workplace was to be a manager. People management, however, has only been my role for some of my career; much of my time has been spent working in teams. My reflection recently has been that leadership and community does not have to be (and probably for most of us isn't) confined to groups of Christians. This, though, is something I have only just realized recently, even though I think I've been doing what I do for years. Leadership and community for many of us is quite often just "being who we are" in our daily lives. For me that is work. I realized that I am able to gather people and grow community at work—in fact I find it easier to do it at work than anywhere else. Considering it is often the place we spend most of our time, I have found it is the place that can often lack community and balance more than anywhere.

This has been something that I was quite worried about when I became a mum. Where would I find people now? Much of my experience and, to a certain extent, my identity was linked to work. Yes, it's been a change; yes, it's been a challenge. But not because community has been hard to find! I've learned again, as I was told in the first place, just to be me, seeking the opportunities that people will gather and follow. Jesus attracts people. We can build community and we can lead, whatever the season. It isn't always obvious, it isn't always (and is sometimes never) at the front, but it is always fun and rewarding and so often surprising. It isn't always big, but just a few people sharing life brings so many opportunities for the kingdom.

Now I'm heading back to work, another new season, and I am excited!

Lizzy Robinson, church leader and mother of three:

Don't try to walk other people's journeys: be yourself and true to who God has made you to be; every person's journey is different.

It can be incredibly helpful to know your gifts and talents, to learn where your skills are best used, to sense where God's Spirit has anointed and empowered you. It's important to try things out, test ideas, get out there and get involved. Yet your effectiveness in leadership is strengthened or seriously undermined by an area of your life that is often overlooked. This area is more important than your gifts, your skill set, your anointing or your opportunities: it's your character. By "character" I mean who you are on the inside, your personality, your emotional maturity, your personal integrity, your attitudes, your values and worldview. Your character carries your strengths and your weaknesses, your wholeness and your brokenness. Your character is shaped by events and experiences, fashioned by your personal relationships, influenced by the culture around you. If we're serious about leadership and godly influence, then we need to pay close attention to our character. We're going to spend a lot of time digging into this subject. Without character we won't have the capacity to handle the testing challenges or even the wonderful opportunities that leadership provides.

With these things in mind, we'll look at the lives of two queens in the Bible and how their character affected their leadership and influence *and* their legacy. We'll experiment with a tool that develops our awareness of what is going on inside our hearts, and helps us see how we deal with the broken pieces of our lives that affect our character. Then we'll look at how some influential female leaders in the Bible worked through challenges and character issues, and see what we can learn from them as we take a closer look at our own lives.

A Tale of Two Queens

*But the LORD said to Samuel, "Do not consider his appearance
or his height, for I have rejected him. The LORD does not look at the
things human beings look at. People look at the outward
appearance, but the LORD looks at the heart."*

1 SAMUEL 16:7 TNIV

*Every time you compromise character
you compromise leadership.*

BILL HYBELS, *COURAGEOUS LEADERSHIP*

JEZEBEL AND ESTHER ARE TWO POWERFUL queens who emerge in the Old Testament for very different reasons. Though dissimilar, leading in different eras and contexts, both women have much to teach us about how the state of our hearts—our character—affects leadership and influence.

Jezebel. When you think of Jezebel, what comes to mind? Manipulative, dominatrix, sexually sated, controlling, evil? How about *broken*? Not a victim, because clearly as an adult she was responsible for the choices she made. But how was her life and marriage and influence shaped by the broken woman she was?

Jezebel was a woman surrounded by power, and yet she started out with a powerless life. She was the daughter of the king of Tyre, yet her value was ignored and her life was controlled from the moment she was born. She was not merely the king's responsibility: she was also his property. So when the time suited the king, she was married off to Ahab, king of Israel, as part of the terms of a political alliance. Now Jezebel was her husband's property.

Ahab was an indulged, self-centered, spoiled man, given to sulking when he didn't get his own way. He was a passive ruler, ready for someone else to be responsible for the challenging decisions that needed to be made. Jezebel finally had the opportunity to do something for herself on her own terms. Power was within reach, so she took it. When she arrived on the scene, she brought with her the gods she worshiped. Her father was not only the king but the high priest of their religion. Jezebel had grown up in it and now it was her turn to take the lead. She brought the worship of Baal (thought to be the lord of the land and rain clouds, and the god of fertility, the weather, etc.) and Asherah (mother goddess of fertility) into Israel. Worship was led by temple priests and temple prostitutes, involving dances and sacred orgies, praying that their gods would make the land more fertile. In times of famine, they slashed wrists, even sacrificed children to get the gods' attention. Despite the fact that Israel had a covenant with the Lord, Ahab failed to model that relationship and acquiesced, building a temple to Baal in Samaria and an Asherah pole (an image of the goddess). Pluralistic values and worship were now officially sanctioned and endorsed, even sponsored, by the royal throne. Then Jezebel brought 450 prophets of Baal and 400 prophets of Ashtoreth (another manifestation of the fertility goddess) from Phoenicia, housed them in the palace and fed them in royal style. Their duties would have been to promote the worship of Baal and Ashtoreth throughout the land.

Elijah, God's prophet, enters the political stage, with a simple prophetic word: God says there will be a famine, no dew, no rain across the land. Then Elijah leaves the country. It's a pronouncement in response to Israel's unfaithfulness, and also a demonstration that

Jezebel's Baal is not as powerful as he seems to be. During the famine, rather than turn back to God, Jezebel kills all of God's prophets she can find, perhaps to appease Baal, to get rain.

Three years after the prophetic word, Elijah returns to Israel and goes to see Ahab. He calls the king, the people and the false prophets to meet on Mount Carmel, to settle once and for all who the true God is. An altar is set up with slain bulls, and whichever deity can set fire to the sacrifice, without human assistance, will be the winner. The prophets of Baal and Asherah scream and shout, even slashing themselves with swords, but nothing happens. Elijah has the altar soaked with water, and then asks God to send fire, reminding the nation of who is the true God. The prophets of Baal are killed, and it looks as though the nation will turn back to God. But Jezebel is not finished. When she hears the news from Mount Carmel, she sends word to Elijah that she will kill him. He runs for his life, collapsing in the wilderness and pleading with God to let him die.

Jezebel is not a woman of empty threats; she uses the power she has to do exactly what she wants. She is manipulative and callous, and in charge. Even of the king.

Ahab sees a vineyard next to his land at his residence in Jezreel. Thinking that it could be a great vegetable garden, he asks Naboth, the owner, to sell it to him or exchange it for another. But Naboth refuses to give up the land because it is more than mere property. "The LORD forbid that I should give you the inheritance of my fathers," he says (1 Kings 21:3). Jezebel later finds Ahab sulking and refusing to eat because Naboth has turned him down (!) and, incredulous at Ahab's response, deals with the situation herself. She frames Naboth and has him and his sons taken out of the city and stoned. There are now no heirs to the estate, so Jezebel tells Ahab he can have the land that he wants. For his vegetable garden.

Jezebel, a broken woman, oppressed all her life, was no longer anybody's property. *She* was the power behind the throne. She would never be controlled again. The results were devastating.[1]

Esther. When you think of Esther, what comes to mind? Beautiful, favored, an influential queen? How about orphaned, stolen, used? King Xerxes, the ruler of the Persian Empire, was powerful, and not only did he know it, he wanted to celebrate it. So he spent six months with his officials and leaders, showing off the splendor and might of his empire. At the end of that time, all the men of Susa, Xerxes' royal city, were invited to seven days of celebrations in the palace gardens. The gardens were richly ornamented, with couches laden with gold and silver, and the best wine flowed in golden goblets. The king issued one command for this event: each man was to drink as much as he liked. His only stipulation was that there were no limitations. And why not? Xerxes was the king of the world.

On the seventh day, Xerxes instructed his officials to summon his wife, Queen Vashti, to the party. She was to wear her royal crown and appear before the drunken king and his (most probably) drunken company. They'd seen his vast wealth. They'd known his power and glory. Now it was time for them to see his wife, "in order to display her beauty to the people and nobles, for she was lovely to look at" (Esther 1:11).

Queen Vashti, who had been acting as hostess to the women at the palace during this time, refused to appear. She said no. And in that one word she ignited a political crisis. Determined that women throughout the empire would not follow the queen's example, Xerxes banished her. That would teach the women of the empire their place.

In time, the king's advisors suggested that Xerxes might undertake an empire-wide search to find a new queen. Young women throughout the empire were taken from their homes, their families, their lives, and swept away into the king's palace. There, after a year of beauty treatments in the king's harem, they would spend one night with Xerxes (no, not talking) to see if they might be the one to be crowned queen. If they weren't, they would return to the harem, now to become one of the king's many, many concubines.

Hadassah was an orphan, adopted by her cousin Mordecai, and part of the Jewish community living in exile in the Persian Empire. (The

Jews were exiled. Israel had succumbed generations earlier to the Babylonians, who in turn had been conquered by the Persians. Jerusalem had been restored to the Jews, but only 50,000 of them had returned.) Not even Mordecai could protect Hadassah from being swept into King Xerxes' story, but Hadassah was not completely alone. She somehow found favor in the horrendous environment, and was looked after by Hegai, supervisor to the concubines. Furthermore, Mordecai her cousin visited the harem courtyard daily to see how she was. He advised her to keep her nationality a secret (perhaps to protect her against discrimination?) so she used another name—Esther.

When her night arrived, the king was drawn to Esther more than to any other woman, and so gave her Vashti's crown: Hadassah the exiled orphan was now Esther the celebrated queen of the Persian Empire. Xerxes hosted a great banquet in her honor and pronounced a public holiday. Perhaps the king's advisors breathed a sigh of relief. Vashti who? Esther is now The One. Maybe it was no fairy tale, but perhaps it would lead to a happily ever after.

Except it wasn't quite that. What does Esther do when she becomes queen? How does she use her new position for influence for the greater good? Well, the truth is that, initially, she doesn't. She does nothing; she simply fits into the world around her, where her beauty, popularity and compliance define her existence and purpose. Theologians sometimes compare her to other young leaders in a similar predicament, God-followers in a foreign land—like Joseph in Egypt or Daniel, Shadrach, Meshach, and Abednego in Babylon— who took a stand for what they believed in, often at great risk. They wonder what went wrong in Esther's case. It's not completely clear, but what we do know is that "she shed her Jewish name, concealed her true identity, and morphed into the surrounding culture."[2] Where was her demonstration of loyalty to God and his values? Did she lose her focus in that year of preparation in the harem, and think that her life was really about her beauty? Did she get comfortable in the palace and simply enjoy the life she now had?

Reality finally confronts Esther when Mordecai clashes with the king's senior advisor, Haman. Haman's antagonism toward Mordecai is so great that Mordecai's death alone would not be enough. He wants to wipe out Mordecai's people, the Jews. So he deceives the king into issuing an edict that would result in the genocide of the Jewish people. The Jewish community is devastated, fearful, in mourning. Mordecai clothes himself in sackcloth and ashes and walks through the city, wailing. Esther sends a messenger to find out what has happened and discovers word of Haman's evil plot. But there is something else. Mordecai tells Esther to go to the king and plead for mercy for the Jewish people.

So how does Esther respond in this desperate moment of crisis? Well, she reminds Mordecai that she's not seen the king for a month, and that it's common knowledge that to approach Xerxes uninvited would result in death unless the king deigned to show mercy. She suggests that there is nothing she can do about the situation. That she, Esther, the queen of Persia, is powerless. She is unable to see beyond her own experiences. She does not have the strength of character to fight for what she believes in, to have an opinion, not even to save the man who adopted her and raised her. And so her initial response to Mordecai's desperate cries for help is to say no (Esther 1–4).

BROKEN HEARTS, BROKEN LEADERS, BROKEN DECISIONS

What went wrong? Jezebel is clearly a strong and accomplished leader. She is effectively the high priestess of her religion. She has literally hundreds of leaders who work for her and are led by her. She is a woman who is not afraid to make decisions and get the job done. But she is also completely messed up. Her life and her leadership appear to be one huge reaction to her personal experiences as an oppressed woman. Her ambition has no boundaries; she'll take power at any price. Jezebel's broken past motivates and shapes the leader she becomes, the decisions that she makes. Her skills are consumed by the depths of brokenness and sin that rage within her heart.

In Esther's case we know we've not seen the full story and the woman she eventually chooses to become. Still, let's take a closer look at her in this moment. What went so wrong that Esther doesn't immediately get involved? Has she bought into the idea that her purpose really is to be just a pretty face, and made something of a truce with the ideals and values that objectified her? Maybe she's simply used to being compliant now. Whatever the reason, the potential that lies deep within Esther remains dormant for as long as she chooses not to engage with what is really happening in the world around her, and with what is happening inside her.

For both of these queens, the nature and effectiveness of their leadership influence is not determined by their skills and talents, or even by the opportunities given them. It's determined by what is happening in their hearts. It's true for us too.

FIRM FOUNDATIONS?

As we step into the life God's called us to, it's essential to know what truly matters to him. We catch a glimpse of God's priorities when he sends Samuel to Bethlehem to anoint a new king who will replace Saul. When Samuel meets the family of Jesse, intending to anoint a king to replace Saul, he is initially drawn to the young men in Jesse's family who look impressive. Aware that Israel's king will be a military leader as Saul has been, he is looking for someone who looks tall, strong and imposing. Eliab, the eldest member of the family, appears to be the obvious choice. Until God speaks:

> But the LORD said to Samuel, "Do not consider his appearance or his height, for I have rejected him. The LORD does not look at the things human beings look at. People look at the outward appearance, but the LORD looks at the heart." (1 Samuel 16:7 TNIV)

We know the story; Samuel goes on to select David, the one out in the fields tending to the sheep. The one they forgot to even mention to Samuel. That's how significant he was! But God saw him, out in the fields, and not only that, saw what truly mattered to him when it came to leadership: that David was a man after God's own heart (1 Samuel 13:14).

It's not that our gifts and talents, our opportunities, our potential influence, our position or role are insignificant. But we'll need more than this if we are going to be leaders. *We need whole and healthy hearts.* Why? Well, in part it's because our loving heavenly Father wants this for all his children, regardless of who or what we become. But in terms of leadership and influence, it's also because if your calling was a building, then the state of your heart functions like the foundations. If they are whole and strong, then the building stands firm, no matter what happens. If the foundations are broken, rotten, weak or incorrectly positioned, the building is already vulnerable. The foundations compromise the whole building. It could crumble around you, leaving nothing but dust and rubble. If we are serious about embracing God's life for us, we need to both look at and invest in our foundations—our hearts. Our gifts, roles and opportunities won't hide our weaknesses, not forever. On the contrary, in the end they often reveal who we truly are. We'll express our hearts in our speech, attitudes, choices, relationships and roles.

HOW'S YOUR HEART?

When we think of the heart today, we often think of our emotions and passions and dreams. The biblical understanding of the word "heart"—*lev* in Hebrew, *kardia* in Greek—is much more expansive than that. In Scripture, the heart encompasses more than our emotions and ideals, though it certainly includes them. The heart also refers to our thoughts, understanding, intellect, will: those things at our very core that motivate and compel us—our personality. According to the biblical worldview, the heart is the seat of our appetites and even our courage.

Jezebel's heart was shaped in response to oppressive relationships, a thirst for power and control, and her refusal to surrender herself wholeheartedly to God. Esther's heart was shaped by the broken circumstances that surrounded her. But she was also shaped by her passivity as she complied with her culture without question and bought into the values of the world around her.

> **Q. Have you paid attention to how your heart is doing?**
>
> **How are you feeling? What thoughts go through your mind? What motivates and compels you? What are you dreaming of or despairing about? What determines your will? What is shaping your heart?**

In many ways these women are extraordinary, but they are ordinary women just like you and me. Our hearts have also been shaped both positively and negatively by relationships in our lives. And when a relationship has a negative effect, it casts a shadow that makes us unable to see situations or people clearly. It's inevitable, then, that it will affect how we lead. And we too have character flaws, weaknesses that threaten the life that God's called us to. We too have attitudes and expectations that muddy our motives and determine our choices. There are still areas of our lives that we find difficult to surrender completely to God. Instead we wrestle them to the ground, struggling with our wants and ways, unable to let go. And there are certainly times when we've paid obeisance to certain cultural values because it's been easier than taking a stand. We've tried to blend into the background, wishing the challenges of responsibility on to someone else, somewhere else. We've all backed out on our call to lead at some point. The only place that we get to point the finger is in the mirror. And while we're there, we should take a long hard look at ourselves. We need to ask ourselves some uncomfortable questions, to get to the heart of the matter. This is not because we want to

condemn ourselves or live in perpetual introspection, but because
we can find out in advance the things within us and around us that
could bring a halt to the life God has for us. And by his grace and the
power of the Spirit, we can be prepared for the struggles and learn to
live a different way.

Reflections on Leadership

Marie Hobbs is an ordained minister with British Assemblies of
God, and she holds a master's degree in missional leadership. She
has been involved in various positions of Christian leadership since
1995. In 2009 Marie Hobbs and Vic Ready planted a new church
in Queenshills, Norwich, and this is where Marie and her husband, Dan, are currently based. Marie reflects on her call to leadership and some lessons learned on her journey:

*For me the call to Christian leadership happened at the age of thirteen. I
had recently become a Christian through a school assembly. I went from
being a very shy girl, lacking in confidence, to a girl who felt a call to
preach and lead. I was stirred by the words of Moses to Joshua, "Be strong
and courageous, because you will lead these people to inherit the land I
swore to their forefathers to give them" (Joshua 1:6). As a young girl I had
struggled with feelings of rejection due to my birth father leaving the family
unit when I was young. My teenage years were also quite volatile and I
often felt very inadequate to respond to God's call. However, the words of
Jeremiah 1:5 would comfort me: "Before I formed you in the womb I knew
you, before you were born I set you apart." I've now been a Christian
twenty-four years, and on my leadership journey there have definitely been
some highs and some lows. I have learnt many lessons along the way and I
am still learning—leaders are always learning.*

*In the early years of being a Christian leader I would regularly say to
God, "Why didn't you just make me a man—then this whole area of*

leadership would have been a lot easier!" In those early years I came across quite a bit of prejudice against female leaders. As a result of this, I felt the need to defend myself and prove my call to others. I became very driven and worked very hard, subconsciously believing I had to be better than all the guys around me. Over the years, however, I have come to realize that I have nothing to prove! I no longer spend huge amounts of time trying to persuade people that I'm called—instead I just get on with it as best I can. I have come to realize that it's really important that we find our security in God, rather than what people say or think about us. Does knowing that mean that things are always easy? No, I still find it at times a little awkward when I attend leaders' meetings and I'm the only woman there or when people are dismissive of my position—but rather than defending or retreating, I have found you just have to keep doing the things you believe God is calling you to do. Fear and intimidation will try to paralyze you, but you must choose to resist them and continually ask God to make you more secure in His love.

Susan Martens Miller, author, wife, mother, lay leader in her church:

Be self-smart. Know yourself. Not everyone is self-smart any more than everyone is music-smart or numbers-smart. For some people, this is more intuitive than it is for others, but everyone can learn. Realize you may have some things to discover about yourself and how these traits affect you in a leadership role. Perhaps you're a people-pleaser. Perhaps you second-guess your own decisions a lot. Perhaps you're impatient with other people who are still processing what seems obvious to you. Maybe you're a scheduler. Maybe you're spontaneous. Label these things for yourself and consider how the traits impact your leadership, for good or for ill.

Coming to a Halt

Who is your toughest leadership challenge? You.

BILL HYBELS,
COURAGEOUS LEADERSHIP

"WHAT WAS YOUR GREATEST MORAL FAILURE?" It was the first time I had met this group of leaders (male and female). Over the next three months we'd have a shared conference call every week for an hour. My job was to coach them about discipleship and introduce them to a few helpful biblical principles. Over time we'd share our stories and support and encourage one another, forging lasting friendships. But this was week one, the setting-the-tone, not-sure-how-this-is-going-to-go week, the getting-to-know-you week. Only I wasn't prepared for quite how deeply known. I couldn't even tell if the question was a joke or not, and I didn't have the time to create an oblique answer. I was instantly reminded of one situation. I don't know if it was my greatest failure, but it was the most memorable one.

"I once preached with a hangover," I said. Sometimes in the silence you can hear people gasp.

I was eighteen years old. It was a significant year. My eighteenth birthday was the start of new freedom and independence for me, in part because in England it's legal to drink alcohol starting at age eighteen. But I was also preparing to leave home. I'd grown an unexpected inch and lost some weight. A summer job, new clothes, a rocking hairstyle, and my confidence was growing. I'd even found that men had begun to notice me, an exhilarating feeling. Alongside that my relationship with God was stagnating. I'd known him since I was nine, and I wasn't going to pretend he didn't exist. I was active in the life of the church; I'd been given opportunities to lead worship, pray, even preach. But now God felt like a childhood friend I was embarrassed to know, the friend who made inappropriate references to what you were like as a child, and didn't seem to fit today. I kept it quiet, though, because I didn't know what to say. I loved my brave new world. I finally fit in, but what would I do with the old Christian one? I decided to do both. So one Sunday morning I stood up after a particularly intoxicating night and tried to preach as though everything was normal. But it so wasn't. It was painful and it was bad. I wasn't sure who noticed, but I felt too embarrassed to talk to my childhood Friend. That morning seemed to summarize that period of my life—or should I say lives, because I lived a double one that year. I used to love the Bible. I used to think preaching was an awesome privilege, and I'd spend hours reading commentaries and different translations and praying. But that was a world away. When I dared to think about it, I now saw that anything and everything I did at church was hollow and fake. I may have appeared to be going through the motions, but my heart was at a standstill.

HALT

HALT—Hungry, Angry, Lonely, Tired—is an acronym used in recovery groups and stress management classes as a self-assessment tool to equip people to be aware of their basic needs and vulnerabilities. In our case we'll use the acronym as a tool to discover the state of our hearts. We may discover some things that we don't want to admit about ourselves; we may find we reconnect with past or present hurts, or have to face wounds or failures. None of these are areas that we feel as leaders we want to face; we're leaders, mothers, leaders' wives, executives—we're the strong ones, we should be over this stuff. We're used to looking out for, looking after, other people;

being the strong shoulder, the confidante, the wise sage. And sometimes it makes us very bad at admitting our own vulnerabilities—particularly to ourselves. But we need to go there. Not in some self-flagellating, weird, condemning way (there's no condemnation for those who are in Christ Jesus [Romans 8:1]!), but because when we bring our brokenness into the light, its grip is loosened and we give God the opportunity to work on us.

So let's use the HALT acronym together, slowly and with raw honesty, allowing God to shine his light on our lives when necessary. Take time over the questions; get a journal to write down your answers. Look at the questions with a close friend. As we begin, let's use David's words from Psalm 139 as our prayer:

> Investigate my life, O God,
>   find out everything about me;
> Cross-examine and test me,
>   get a clear picture of what I'm about;
> See for yourself whether I've done anything wrong—
>   then guide me on the road to eternal life.
>   (Psalm 139:23-24 *The Message*)

HUNGRY

What do you do when you are hungry? The most obvious answer is *eat*, isn't it? But what do we eat, and how much do we eat? Sometimes we eat food as fuel for our bodies, as a God-given resource to celebrate and enjoy. But there are other times when we have an interesting *relationship* with food. Food becomes our comfort and our company on sad or stress-filled days, meeting a deeper need than we would like to admit. Sometimes food is our enemy that we interact with in fear or resentment, or seek to avoid as much as possible. We may have struggled with our certain habits for years. We may still be significantly affected by the airbrushed images of our culture that have limited our understanding of beauty.

Q. What do your eating habits say about you? What do
your drinking habits say about you?

What hidden habits do you use in an attempt to satisfy
your hungers?

Sometimes our hunger is not just physical but actually reflects deeper
longings. We may hunger for love, approval and acceptance. We may
hunger for recognition and influence and power. These longings become particularly poignant for us as leaders when we've experienced a
lack of recognition of our gifts and watched as opportunities we were
qualified for have been handed over to others. Sometimes that's simply
because someone else is actually the right person for the job and, painful
though it is, we have to learn to accept that. Sometimes, though . . .

What do you do when you hunger for approval and acceptance?
It's a longing that probably started long ago, long before you were a
leader. It could have started when you were a young child in your
family, in your relationship with parents or siblings. It could have
started in the school playground when you felt or were told that you
just didn't fit in. Wherever it began, now that hunger seeps into the
woman you've become and influences your areas of influence. You
work hard in your sphere—be it the office, the church, your community—hoping that you will be valued for your contribution. We'll
call it serving others, but in certain instances it's actually fulfilling
your own need. We all need to be needed. You might even work too
hard, lacking boundaries, unable to say no to anything, hoping to
earn your way into acceptance and perhaps new opportunities. It's
disappointing, frustrating, when it seems to make little difference.

What do you do when you hunger for recognition and influence
and power? Remember Jezebel? Let's return to her story. After she has
Naboth killed and gives his land to Ahab, Elijah comes and prophesies
God's judgment on the king and queen (1 Kings 21:19, 23-24). Ahab

finally humbles himself before God, repentant, but it appears that Jezebel remains defiant. The final time we see Jezebel in Scripture, many years have passed. Ahab is dead, and has been succeeded first by his son Ahazariah, then by another son, Jehoram. Jehoram was a king as corrupt as his father, married to Athaliah, a woman who functioned much like Jezebel. Elijah has been taken up to heaven, and Elisha is now the nation's main prophetic voice. Elisha sends a young man from his prophetic team to anoint Jehu king, and commission him as king to deal with Ahab's family and bring about the judgment that Elijah had prophesied years before. Jehu kills Jehoram and, in a twist of irony and justice, has his body dumped in Naboth's vineyard. When Jehu arrives at Jezreel, Jezebel knows her time has come.

> When Jezebel heard that Jehu had arrived in Jezreel, she made herself up—put on eyeshadow and arranged her hair—and posed seductively at the window. When Jehu came through the city gate, she called down, "So, how are things, 'Zimri,'[1] you dashing king-killer?" (2 Kings 9:30-31 *The Message*)

Jezebel had been the power behind the throne for decades and was politically savvy enough to know that a woman with her degree of influence and power would not survive. Yet she uses her sexuality as a weapon—her make-up, her look, a seductive pose and a sharp tongue—to either save herself or as one final defiant statement. She dies anyway. Nonetheless, it's a powerful lasting image of a woman who has gone to incredible lengths to secure power throughout her life. She will use violence, she will use manipulation, and she'll use her sexuality.

In today's sex-saturated culture, it seems that the messages we receive are that sex is one of the ways to get what we want, to get where we want. You even find that things that were once associated with the objectification of women, like poles usually found in strip clubs, are sometimes described as liberating or empowering, and a reflection of a woman's free choice to express herself as she wants. I'm all for freedom of expression, but I'm not convinced that this is truly redemptive. But to return to our hunger for recognition and influence—Jezebel's final moments used sexuality as a tool for her influence (as indeed did the religious practices she promoted in the nation).

STANDING HER GROUND

Lucy was an up-and-coming management trainee in an international company. She was young, incredibly competent and motivated. Her mentor, Greg, was a much admired and respected executive in the company. His connections and endorsement had the power to propel a career to new heights. She enjoyed learning from him and working with him. One weekend on a business trip, the tone changed. Though he was much older than she was, he began to flirt with her, and made it very clear that he wanted to sleep with her. As a committed Christian, Lucy had already resolved in her heart that if she was to advance in the company it would be through merit, not through sexual encounters with powerful men. But on this occasion she felt that she needed to make a public stand for her faith as well. She told him simply and politely that she was a Christian and that she wasn't prepared to sleep with him, even if it meant it would affect her career. Greg was completely taken aback.

"Wow!" he responded quietly. "I wish I could say that my daughters would respond just like you did in this situation."

> Q. What role, if any, does sexual politics play in your professional advancement?
>
> Where are you tempted to use your sexuality—when hungry for influence or power?

It might be in a lingering touch, flirtatiousness, the coquettish smile. It might be that you know that there's a certain outfit that's not just attractive but shows a little more leg, reveals a little more information on top! It might be that in your marriage, sex (or the lack thereof!) is how you manage to secure some degree of influence. What's the big deal with a little harmless flirtation? It's always been the way you could get what you wanted or needed. It's nothing really. Really.

Really?

Finally as we talk about hungers and sexuality, we have to acknowledge that women have sexual appetites, separate from appetites rooted in a longing for acceptance, approval or a quest for control. We're designed for intimate relationship. We know that as Christians we're called to celibacy outside marriage and fidelity within, but temptation affects all of us. Leadership and influence can be a giddy environment; the leader is often the center of attention. People are drawn to leaders simply because they are attracted to power. We need to pay attention, observing not just how people treat us but what this awakens within our hearts.

> These dynamics will not change anytime soon. Temptations will continue to challenge our inner discipline and put our anchors to the test. We need to know better the sexually provocative nature of leadership and authority.[2]

ANGRY

What happens when you're angry? We get angry for all kinds of reasons; an injustice, a misunderstanding, broken relationships and missed opportunities. Anger seems to be an inevitable part of our lives. Getting angry is not an automatic indicator of sin—though, knowing the nature of the human heart only too well, Scripture advises us not to let our anger lead us toward sin (Ephesians 4:26). Anger is a topic that we often find uncomfortable, because many of us are uncomfortable with conflict. Maybe for us it feels unchristian, even unfeminine. And as female leaders the last thing we want to appear as is aggressive. We'll even avoid the word, saying we "struggle" with something or "find it difficult" rather than saying we're angry with someone. Yet we ignore anger at our own peril. Anger is an indicator that something somewhere needs to be resolved, and in its own way it is relentless in its demand for attention.

When we fail to deal with anger, it stagnates into unforgiveness and bitterness, which in turn produce their own pungent toxins like cynicism and sarcasm. Alternatively, we can try to suppress anger with a polite (if somewhat strained) smile. We internalize it, wishing it away, but often it results in disillusionment and despair. Sadly, its impact overflows into our everyday lives. Problems remain unresolved, and relationships are neglected or maintained with a degree of emotional distance. These things begin to define and reshape us. Our relationships suffer, our work suffers, and our walk with God, the kingdom, suffers.

> Q. So what do you do when you are angry—do you internalize it, or do you lash out?
>
> How does anger affect your capacity to lead in the position God has given you? How does it shape your influence?

Perhaps you speak negatively about other work colleagues in the presence of those you lead. Do you become particularly competitive with certain people? Do you become less of a team player? Do you reveal information given in confidence? Or take secret pleasure when you hear someone is not doing as well as you?

These are horrible things to think about, aren't they? None of us wants to be that person! No one ever wants to admit feelings like this, especially when you have a leadership role. But not wanting these feelings is not the same as not having them. We've all been there; some of us are still there, on occasions. We need to admit these things so that we are not held captive to them. The beauty of a life with Jesus is that no matter how wrong we've been, by his grace we don't have to stay there.

A psychologist friend of mine helpfully pointed out to me once that anger is a secondary emotion. She said it was a symptom, a response to fear or hurt.

A thousand little cuts to the heart. Claire preached her first sermon at her church; she was encouraged when a woman offered to
pray with her afterward. Preaching was something she was just step-
ping into, something her senior pastor had endorsed and encouraged. Her sense of encouragement began to drain away when the
woman prayed that Claire would learn to be more submissive to her
husband and be silent.

Sharon, a church planter, was excited at the chance to get away on
retreat with her husband and spend time with other leaders. But she
was unsure how to process her sense of alienation when everyone
assumed that her husband was the pastor and seemed to ignore her.
When people realized she was actually the pastor, it appeared to be a
real conversation-killer! Was she being too sensitive? Or was their
presumption offensive?

The first time I encountered difficulties as a female leader was as
member of a mission team serving a local church. My team leader
had given me the task of preaching at our host church on that Sunday
morning. When the service was about to start, the minister of the
church walked into the room and grumbled, "When they told me a
Jo was preaching, I thought that would be a Joseph!" I was nineteen
or twenty, sassy with a touch of arrogance. I smiled and said, "There's
only one Jo here and I'm a Joannah," as he left the room, clearly
unhappy about the situation.

Over the years there have been many different challenges to navigate. The self-protective sassiness from my former years that used to
help me bounce back has proved insufficient as I have grown older.
I didn't want to be sassy; I just wanted to get on with what I felt
called to be and do. Still, it wasn't straightforward. Words, events,
actions began to penetrate, then hurt. There was the time when I
was told that men didn't like strong women, and that being a leader
made me pretty inaccessible to the opposite sex. My heart interpreted it to mean that if I wanted to settle down, I needed to—well,
settle down! Be less outspoken and forthright. Be less visible, lead

less. Later, as a married woman, I noted how I would be ignored and overlooked. I wondered why. I'd find, when I turned up to meetings, that the first thing I would be asked was where my husband was. Years later I was due to speak at a young adults' conference, but we couldn't find a venue. It came to light that the reason we couldn't find a venue was that the churches were unprepared to host a conference that had a woman speaker. I was relieved when circumstances intervened and I had to step down anyway.

These experiences are like a thousand little cuts to the heart. Tired of bleeding, we become jaded, hardened, isolated, in order to protect ourselves from greater pain.

> Q. **What do we do when we become angry? About leadership concerns, or about anything else?**

We need to be aware of our vulnerabilities so we can bring them to the Father.

LONELINESS

Mother Teresa described loneliness as the worst kind of poverty. Everyone appreciates and benefits from solitude from time to time. We all need space to recharge. But that is not the same as the pervasive sting of loneliness. Loneliness is not just when we find ourselves without company for extended periods, though that can be painful enough. Loneliness can also be found when we're surrounded by company that lacks meaningful relationships with others, when our lives lack intimacy, or when we're the stranger or the minority in a group. What are you more likely to do when you are lonely? Does loneliness thrust us into someone's arms, regardless of whether they are good for us or not, simply because we crave the intimacy? It could send us into a spiral of negative thinking, a pit of deep depression. Or in seeking to escape its grasp, loneliness may drive us toward fantasy, a world of our own construction filled with the quality relationship that we long for. It's not real, but we find the time to daydream. Loneliness gives us successive tear-stained nights and an aching heavy heart. Powerful in its grip, it doesn't leave you with energy for much else.

I wonder if Esther was lonely. Yes, she was surrounded by many women in her position, at least initially. But what was it like to be chosen to be queen? In that moment her life was separated from every woman in the harem. I wonder what the dynamics of her relationships were like. Were the women in the harem still her friends, or were they now a threat to her marriage? What was it like to be married to Xerxes, knowing that his harem existed, having to wait to be summoned before she could see him, talk to him? Furthermore, she was still hiding her secret. No one knew her nationality, that she was Hadassah, one of God's covenant people. I wonder how it felt to be isolated from her covenant community, her cultural traditions and festivals, while being publicly admired and adored for her beauty and her position. She'd won the king's heart (give or take a harem) but at what cost? What had she lost? Thankfully, she had Mordecai. But she didn't have a mother, and every woman needs someone who'll be a sister, who'll remind you of who you are. Perhaps it was inevitable that she became a voiceless beauty.

We know that leadership (inside and outside the church) is costly and lonely for both men and women. Sometimes the position we have and the decisions we make stretch our relationships with our colleagues. For many women in leadership, the cost is intensified by the loneliness they experience because there aren't many women in their position. There is so much to process, but they look at their colleagues, uncertain that they will understand what they are going through. Besides, we have the weighty burden that we women leaders don't represent only ourselves, but any other woman coming after us. No pressure, but don't mess it up so that your behavior becomes a burden for the rest of us. And some things are simply inappropriate to share with the men you work with, and everyone is simply respecting healthy boundaries.

For a friend of mine who's a partner in a law firm, the loneliness stems from being salt and light when she travels to conferences and meetings. She loves her friends and colleagues and enjoys working with them, but she's not prepared to buy into the alcohol-soaked lunches and parties, where her hardworking colleagues start to party hard too. It's certainly part of the package of leadership—so we need to be aware of how it affects us and how we can best respond.

> Q. Is loneliness the cost for female Christian leaders breaking through into positions of influence?
>
> Do you feel the loneliness of leadership?

TIRED

What do you do when you are tired? We know that physical tiredness plays havoc with our effectiveness. When we're overworked and burned out, we can't give our best even if we want to, and that's true of both our work and the relationships that we hold closest to our hearts. Tiredness affects our perspective, our decisions and our capacity to stand under pressure and withstand temptation. Learning how to rest is fundamental for a leader, and we'll explore it in a later chapter. In the meantime, though, let's identify how we function when we're tired. Perhaps we are more sensitive; perhaps we say or do things that we'll regret the next day. It's bizarre to think it may be because we need to go to bed earlier or take a day off. But give it a try, and observe the difference it makes!

In addition to physical tiredness, there's the tiredness that comes from being tired of a situation. The writer of Proverbs notes that hope deferred makes the heart sick (Proverbs 13:12). Are you heartsick? Perhaps we wrestle with unanswered prayer. Has our love for the Lord been eroded by prayers that lie unanswered? How does that affect our leadership and what we say to those we lead and disciple?

We may be tired of a difficult relationship, of financial uncertainty or chronic conditions. What happens when you are tired?

Some of us are beyond tired of the struggle to be accepted and encouraged in leadership. That night at Momentum was one where hundreds of women gave voice to the depth of their struggle, the ocean of their sorrow. Many of us know that even as we read these pages about empowering women for influence, our environment is a struggle. Some of us know we need to be twice as good as the men around us to have a voice and be heard. We know we'll never get a mentor. We have worked extra hard to respond to a sense of calling that is challenged at every turn. We may find ourselves consistently overlooked, patronized for no other reason but our gender. We've been expected to laugh at jokes we don't find funny for the sake of not wanting to appear oversensitive. And we tired of it. Tired of walking on eggshells wherever we work so as not to not let our side (women) down. Tired of the rejection of our gifts, our call and our sacrifice. We're tired of the way our contribution, as mothers, teachers, youth leaders, has not been acknowledged. Tired of the way these things tap into a million other insecurities.

Soon tiredness acts as a trigger to your hungers, your anger, your loneliness—until it brings your life and your calling to a HALT.

The HALT technique is a great way to take a long look at our hearts. It probably won't cover everything, but it's a tool that provides a good place to start. It's not pleasant and it's certainly not comfortable to admit our brokenness and our potential for failure. But comfort is not our primary goal. Our primary goal is to follow Jesus, to embrace the life and freedom that our Savior died for, a life he offers us freely. If the discomfort is the journey to the freedom only Christ can bring, let's take it. And as leaders, let's see this HALT heart check-up as fundamental to our leadership development. We need to be aware so that we can be prepared for the external and internal battles that are an inevitable part of life. As Heifetz and Linsky note, when it comes to leadership, "Self knowledge and self discipline form the foundation of staying alive."[3]

We want to stay alive in leadership, and we want to thrive in the opportunities that the Lord has given us. Looking with HALT reveals our hearts, but is not an end in itself. If it were, we'd all give up leading, paralyzed by our fear of failure! Where do we go with all the things that have come up? We'll explore what to do with what we've discovered in the coming chapters.

Reflections on Leadership

Gareth Robinson, church leader and worship leader:

Put character before gifting. Don't work too hard to prove yourself; center your identity from the Father's love, not the gifts he gave you. Be faithful in the little things and allow the Lord to work on your character, rather than grasping for the greater thing, which would be avoiding the character formation so necessary for the long haul (it's a marathon, not a sprint).

Naomi, a missionary in Mozambique:

We're all in need of more healing. Keep seeking it and go and get prayer/ ministry/talk to the Lord when things come up. Keep seeking more and more freedom. But also know that we won't get it all at once, so learn to be comfortable in your state of not being perfect! Be honest with it, keep talking to him about it. And remember, your status with him is the same. Broken or whole, he loves you just the same!

Sally Breen, 3D Ministries:

A secure sense of our identity in God, knowing his unconditional love as our Father is everything.

Broken in God's House

*The world shouts out negative and harmful messages at us every step
of the way. The devil laughs as we absorb them. Instead we must keep
turning to Jesus to hear his clear voice and the truth about who we are.
We can sit in front of Jesus and cry with the pain of inadequacy
and worthlessness—but if we let him, he will pick us up
again and again and gently set us on our way.*

ALI HERBERT,
"JUST FINISH IT, BABY!"

IT'S CLEAR THEY WILL NEVER BE BEST FRIENDS, but did she
have to be so cruel? Elkanah the Zuphite has two wives. Hannah was
his first wife but she has no children. Then second, both in order and in
Elkanah's affections, is his wife Peninnah, who has given birth to both
sons and daughters. When the family takes an annual trip to Shiloh to
worship God and offer sacrifices, Elkanah gives Hannah particularly
generous portions of the sacrificial meal, more than Peninnah or their
children. It's a small gesture, but one filled with meaning: an acknowl-
edgment of Hannah's position in his affections and her silent pain. Perhaps because of this, Peninnah taunts and mocks Hannah for her infertility, reminding Hannah that God hasn't given Hannah children,
unlike her. This pattern of taunting and ridicule continues for years.

One year, utterly bereft, Hannah can't eat. She has no appetite.
All she can do is cry. Elkanah attempts to comfort and encourage her

with the life she has with him, and in doing so completely misunderstands her grief and her needs in that moment. It's all too much. Hannah leaves and goes to the Lord's house.

There, she is finally able to let go. Deep sobs of anguish well up from within and pour out. Prayers and tears, tears and prayers. Hannah prays the prayer she's always prayed, the one she longs to have answered. This time she makes a vow that, if the Lord gives her a son, that child's life will be dedicated to him. Eli the priest is watching Hannah. He sees her anguished convulsions, her soundless murmurs, and she looks an absolute mess. In public! He assumes she is drunk and challenges her, until she explains.

> Oh no, sir—please! I'm a woman hard used. I haven't been drinking. Not a drop of wine or beer. The only thing I've been pouring out is my heart, pouring it out to GOD. Don't for a minute think I'm a bad woman. It's because I'm so desperately unhappy and in such pain that I've stayed here so long. (1 Samuel 1:15-16 *The Message*)

Eli sends her home in peace, and it's not long after their meeting that Hannah's prayer is answered, first in the form of a baby named Samuel, who will grow up to become the last great judge of Israel, and then in five more children (1 Samuel 1–2).

> Q. **Where do we go when our brokenness rises to the surface, to the point where it overwhelms our lives?**

Hannah was not alone in her situation in the Old Testament, but she seems to handle it differently from other women that we meet there. Sarai has to reconcile her own experience of infertility with God's promises. Her response is to take matters into her own hands by providing Abraham with her maid Hagar to provide a child (Genesis 16). When Hagar becomes pregnant, she begins to despise her mistress. Sarai regrets her decision, and abuses Hagar until she runs away.

Sisters Leah and Rachel compete for their husband, Jacob's, affections for years. Rachel, known for her beauty, was the woman Jacob fell in love with and wanted to marry. Leah, Rachel's older, plainer sister, was acquired as part of the arrangement, through their father Laban's deceptions. The balance of power shifts dramatically when it becomes clear that Leah can have children but Rachel can't. Their brokenness is expressed through the competition to have children, with Rachel in particular resorting to desperate measures to change her life and position.

These stories remind us that brokenness in our own hands can destroy us and ruin those we love and all we live for. In stark contrast, Hannah's story demonstrates what to do with the aspects of HALT that are found in a broken life, and offers us lessons to live by as part of our own leadership journey.

HANNAH'S STORY, OUR JOURNEY

Hannah did not deny the anguish of infertility. She did not pretend that Peninnah's cruelty didn't affect her. She was crushed. Every feature of HALT is evident. There's aching and longing, frustration, loneliness and weariness. There was no denial over the reality of her life and situation and the fact that it desperately hurt her. There were no masks that covered up a painful truth.

Hannah models for us how important it is to be honest about the broken pieces of our lives. Acknowledging the depths of our personal struggles and sorrows as she did is often a significant battle in itself. Hannah did more than own her tears, though. She poured her hurt and her heart in a raw, honest relationship with God. The pressures, the taunts and the misunderstanding concerning infertility drove Sarai to abuse. They drove Rachel to distraction, competition and relying on superstitions rather than God. In contrast, they drove Hannah into the presence of God. God was the safe place for her pain. They also drove her to prayer. Hannah laid hold of God with desperate, honest, bold, audacious prayers. They were prayers asking for a powerful God to move in her life, prayers offering a surrendered heart and life. We don't have to pretend with God: He knows anyway.

Consider what it would be like to make God your safe place. The place you run and hide when accusations and taunting come your way, when misunderstandings bewilder you. And I wonder what prayers you'd pray, whether you'd allow your desperation and pain a voice, and whether you would ask for God to answer you again, whether you'd dedicate your life to him again. Some of us have backed off from our calling because it was just too difficult, frustrating and painful. So we've settled for a version that makes life a bit more tenable. It's a completely understandable response. But there may be some of us, like Hannah, who need to rededicate our lives and let our hearts cry to God again.

Hannah and Eli. Hannah is not alone in God's house. While this is an intensely personal moment, it's not a private one. When Hannah goes to the temple, she will have passed Eli the priest, seated on duty at the entrance of the temple. Two things stand out for us as we deal with our broken lives:

We too approach a Priest. The writer to the Hebrews reminds us:

Therefore, since we have a great high priest who has gone through the heavens, Jesus the Son of God, let us hold firmly to the faith we profess. For we do not have a high priest who is unable to empathize with our weaknesses, but we have one who has been tempted in every way, just as we are—yet he did not sin. Let us then approach the throne of grace with confidence, so that we may receive mercy and find grace to help us in our time of need. (Hebrews 4:14-16)

We may have been hiding in fear and shame, thinking that as leaders, mothers, women we should have been better at life than this. *Surely we should have dealt with that eating problem, fixed that cutting issue, lifted that self-esteem. Come on, you're a leader now, you're a mother now!* Meanwhile our Priest waits for us, with love and understanding. He also offers us the resources to lead us through our situation. It's another reminder, a reassurance that it's right to approach God with all that HALT entails in our lives.

Hannah isn't interested in keeping up appearances. She doesn't change where she is or who she is because of Eli's presence, covering up her life and pain with a mask of strained smiles and platitudes. Even when he judges her and accuses her of drunkenness, Hannah doesn't run away. She may be broken but she is still an *ezer*, she is strong. Through the tears, Hannah respectfully corrects Eli and helps him understand her life and what has brought her to such anguish.

I'm pretty sure I would not have shown Hannah's strength of character in this moment, if I were accused of drunkenness in my moment of need. I think I'd have run away and been wary of visiting the temple again because of the wound left by my leader. It's striking that Hannah is not afraid to be open and transparent in her community, but doesn't act as a victim when she is misunderstood. She humbly stands her ground and makes Eli understand where she is coming from, then draws strength from his support. Hannah perseveres, and Eli becomes her advocate and later an integral part of her answered prayer. *Are we open to God's provision in terms of other people who will help us through our difficulties?* It may be that we need extra prayer support, counseling, someone to talk to who will stand alongside us. Leaders are notorious for supporting other people while failing to reach out for the support that they themselves need. *Are we willing, like Hannah, to press in and persevere for the help we need?* There is a role that our faith community plays in our lives, as God's instrument of healing and empowering, which we'll explore in greater detail in later chapters.

Hannah's example teaches us to embrace our broken lives and allow them to drive us into God's house, the safest place. She reminds us that we can come to God as we are, not as we feel we ought to be, should be. Her words reveal a posture of raw honesty yet total surrender, not cynicism, in her relationship with God. Hannah also reminds us that we can get beyond concerns of what others think of us, working through our brokenness. We can even get past their misunderstanding and accusation, and still lay hold of what God has for our lives.

A few months after the hangover preaching incident, I sat and listened as a preacher asked a few simple questions. She said simply, "Why do you do the things you do? What makes you say the things you say? And why do you live the life you live?" She challenged us to look again at the hidden issues driving our lives. She didn't condemn any behavior, simply reminded us that God was interested in healing the pain that our behavior spoke of. At the end of the service I sat in silence. The tears streaming down my face confessed the double life I'd been leading for so, so long. They washed away the mask I'd been wearing, the smile and the words and the lies, but they couldn't wash away the memories that seemed to be flooding my mind. At some point a woman sat down next to me and asked if she could pray with me. I took a deep breath, turned toward her and said, "The reason why I live the way I do is . . ." And the healing began.

When we look at HALT, our character and our past, we may feel we're like Eve, an *ezer* fallen from grace. There is an alternative to our interior lives being controlled by HALT. There is an alternative to our secret lives giving birth to public failure. It's not easy or pain free. It may be incredibly humbling and drenched with tears. But it's a safe place, because as we embrace who we truly are, we also find ourselves in his embrace, ready to restore us into who we were meant to be.

RESTORED WITH A NEW NAME, TO A TRUE IDENTITY

God also said to Abraham, "As for Sarai your wife, you are no longer to call her Sarai; her name will be Sarah."

GENESIS 17:15

There are a number of occasions in the Bible where God changes or specifically chooses a person's name. Jacob becomes Israel. Abram is now Abraham. In biblical times, a name was so much more than a title. A name encompassed a person's potential, reputation, their character, personality. When you heard someone's name you really did discover who they were. A name would also be an indicator of who they were in relationship with. Today many of us change our names when we enter the covenant of marriage. It reveals our new identity and expresses the level of commitment we've made to this particular relationship. The people of the biblical world were covenant-making people, but not just with marriage. Covenants were made between friends (think David and Jonathan) and people groups, where a greater party (e.g., a king) invited a lesser party into covenant relationship. These relationships were confirmed in blood (a sacrificed animal) and evidenced by a scar. The weaker party would give up their old identity and receive the identity of their new partner—along with their resources, benefits and protection. And the greater covenant partner also gave the lesser partners their name.

When God confirms his covenant with Abram, Abram and his wife are renamed. Scholars note that God takes the two Hs from his name, YHWH, and inserts them into Abram and Sarai, transforming their identities. Abram—whose name meant "exalted father"—becomes Abraham, "father of many." Sarai, whose name means "princess," is also changed and becomes Sarah. Sarai had lived with another label, another name. No matter what her contribution to her community, she was defined by a bigger label: barren (Genesis 11:30). This was the label that shaped her life, her worth, her value and the choices she made. Still God renames her Sarah, now calling her "the mother of nations" (Genesis 17:16), and in doing so gives her a new identity. Now that his power and his resources are part of her life, transformation is near—and even miracles. Through God's power, Sarah's potential can become a reality.

This covenant pattern continues into the New Testament where Jesus gave Peter a new name, "the rock," and so redefined his life and his calling as a leader. Peter, like Sarah, like Abraham and others, certainly made some mistakes. Still, in time and by God's power, Peter learned to live out who Jesus said he was.[1]

Are you tired of where you've been and who you've become in your life? You started out well, but along the way you lost sight of who God called you to be. Or are you bound by labels that define and restrict you? Labels like "not feminine enough," because of your leadership role. There is still hope for you and me. Jesus is *our* stronger covenant partner. He was the sacrifice. He bore, still bears, the scars. He took our old labels, the mistakes, the wounds, upon himself and they died with him. On the cross a beautiful, powerful redemptive exchange takes place. While Hannah teaches us we can approach God boldly with our lives as we are, Sarah reminds us that so great is his unfailing love that God has taken the initiative to reach us and redefine our lives. We may have failed, we may be broken, but God restores us.

> Q. Have you experienced God's restoration and healing?
> How has it affected the way you lead?

Karen had been a church leader for many years. A visionary, Karen was always looking for innovative ways to reach out to the community. She was an academic, an incredible thinker. The one thing that she knew she couldn't comprehend was God's love. Karen often felt she had to prove herself to God; she couldn't quite connect with him as Father. Her own father loved her but was distant. In response she'd worked extra hard all her life to make him notice her. She expected God to be the same. One day as she prayed about God restoring her identity and her relationship with him, she felt that God gave her the name Elizabeth. She looked up Elizabeth in the

Bible, but didn't identify with her at all. Karen wondered why she wasn't given a name like Deborah or Priscilla, a leader in the Bible whose characteristics she could identify with! But the name just wouldn't go away. When she explored the name Elizabeth, she found a number of meanings: "God's oath," "God's promise", "the fullness of God," "consecrated to God," even "I am God's daughter."

"It changed everything," said Karen. "It's changed how I pray, how I read the Bible, how I lead. Before this there was uncertainty. Now I know God loves me and I'm doing his work. I'm part of the family. He's my Father."

Even members of Karen's congregation noticed a change in her. Karen led with a renewed confidence and clarity—not because she relied on her many considerable gifts or because she worked extra hard because she had so much to prove, but because now she led from a place of greater wholeness and security. She stood in her God-given authority and relied on his power. And her covenant partner was with her, transforming her community. We can start again: the Lord gives us a new name, a new identity, releasing us to be the leaders God created us to be!

HEART HEALTHY

We've looked at how to attend to the broken areas of our lives. It's also important to explore practical ways to help our hearts stay healthy, and develop and strengthen our character. A few suggestions, beginning with the biblical caution to guard your heart:

> Above all else, guard your heart,
> for everything you do flows from it. (Proverbs 4:23 TNIV)

We know that our hearts are shaped by numerous things, so it's important that we learn how to guard them.

First, spend some time *observing the culture in which you live.* Observe the messages that it sends to women about their worth and value, their significance and the conditions of their acceptance. Take note of the messages communicated about women, about leadership, about Christianity, in the magazines and books you read, the TV shows and movies you watch, the music you listen to—our culture's communicators. Then spend some time thinking about how those messages influence you. Are they affecting body image, tapping into hidden insecurities, drawing you into particular value systems that contradict the covenant relationship that you are in? If any of these things are shaping our hearts, we need to explore how to guard against it. I'm not suggesting that we cut off all contact from society at large, its media and people. That's just weird. However, I am asking: if there are things in our lives that feed our hearts with junk and then we feel like junk, what's going on? The media and the arts offer us so much in the form of entertainment—such creativity! Still, we may need to learn how to critique the cultural messages around them, rather than passively be discipled by them.

Guarding our hearts sounds a little reactionary and defensive. But we guard our hearts by cultivating a healthy relationship with the Lord. This isn't limited to developing spiritual disciplines; it also concerns embracing some fundamental principles in our lives. Our hearts are protected when we learn how to surrender ourselves to God fully, to die to ourselves. This, after all, is what Jesus invited us to when he called his disciples then and now to pick up our cross and daily follow him. It protects our hearts from the snare of ambition and entitlement. Our dreams and our appetites are not permitted to become our rights. There is room for more humility in our lives. We're protected when we learn how to practice forgiveness and release those who have hurt us with peace and blessing. They no longer owe us anything. Our hearts are shielded by the choice to be thankful. We're not in denial about tough times, though it's healthy for the heart to be honest about our pain. Instead we choose to be thankful in everything because he is still God.

We learn how to make more room for God in our lives. If God's words to us are more fundamental to our survival than food (Matthew 4:4), we need to craft our lives to make room to hear his voice. Are we reading the Bible regularly, and meeting Jesus there? Are we praying? Are we spending time in worship and adoration, confession and repentance? Do we tithe, do we fast? Are we continually being filled with the Spirit as Scripture calls us to be (Ephesians 5:18)?[2] Do we take the opportunity to retreat from the demands of our lives and be with the Lord, to listen to him, to take note of and respond to what he has to say to our lives? Obviously this isn't about achieving God's approval and love—the cross expressed God's love for us before we even knew God's name. But to sustain and cultivate any close relationship we need to invest in it, even sacrifice for it, as a tangible expression of our love. These are some of the ways Jesus invites us to do the same. If you're looking for more ideas, check out *Real God, Real Life* and see what inspires you!

PEOPLE POWER

Not all of our character development takes place in isolation. Remember Queen Esther? She is the passive beauty who initially seems powerless when her people are threatened with genocide. Initially she says she can do nothing to help, even though she is married to the most powerful man in the Persian Empire, Xerxes himself, saying,

> All the king's officials and the people of the royal provinces know that for any man or woman who approaches the king in the inner court without being summoned the king has but one law: that they be put to death unless the king extends the gold scepter to them and spares their lives. But thirty days have passed since I was called to go to the king. (Esther 4:11 TNIV)

A mere five verses later, though, she says this:

> Go, gather together all the Jews who are in Susa, and fast for me. Do not eat or drink for three days, night or day. I and my

attendants will fast as you do. When this is done, I will go to
the king, even though it is against the law. And if I perish, I
perish. (Esther 4:16 TNIV)

We know that one man was the catalyst for this sudden transformation in Esther: her cousin Mordecai. Maybe it wasn't sudden; Mordecai knows Esther better than anyone—he raised her as his own
child. Perhaps he's seen her potential for a long time. Because of the
depth of their relationship, Mordecai can say things to Esther that no
one else can. Now is the moment. So he challenges Esther to her core
and ignites her heart. Suddenly Esther is a spiritual leader, calling a
nation of people to prayer and fasting. Now Esther is ready and willing to lay down her life for her people. She is bold, she is courageous,
and now she is walking in a different kind of power. Whether Mordecai was drawing out of Esther something he had already seen
within her, or whether his words were sheer desperation, the fact
remains that Esther was transformed in and by a relationship, her
community. Through conversation with her cousin, Esther chose to
engage with her calling and realize her God-given potential.

We often perceive that leadership is a lone pursuit, isolated from
others, somewhat detached. Though leadership can be lonely sometimes, relationships still have a significant role to play in our growth
as leaders. Like Mordecai and Esther, our relationships can wake us
up to who we really are and point us to where we need to be. They
can be life-giving, healing, encouraging, catalysts for growth. We
explore them in the next chapter.

Reflections on an Influential Life

Josephine, married to a curate and bringing up three gorgeous children:

*Leadership is challenging. And challenges that are overwhelming to one
seem insignificant to another, who in turn is probably struggling with
something completely different—all of which probably boils down to our*

personal sense of identity and security. I think that the enemy uses whatever means he can to undermine God's calling on our lives.

Fuzz Kitto, church leader and consultant:

1. *Know who you are and whose you are and the gifts/strengths/talents you have to offer, and develop and grow these.*

2. *Build your character and faith so you develop resilience and emotional intelligence.*

3. *Team with others and do not deny yourself the wellsprings that give you energy, strength and joy.*

Influential Relationships

If I have seen a little further it is by standing on the shoulders of Giants.

Sir Isaac Newton

There's a special place in hell for women who don't help other women.

Madeleine Albright, former U.S. Secretary
of State and Ambassador to the UN

Esther's story would not be complete without the love and the challenge of her cousin Mordecai. His influence completely transformed her life. Without him she simply would not have made it. It's a pattern we see throughout the Bible; where or even *who* would Barak be without Deborah? Or Ruth be without Naomi, Samuel without Eli, David without Jonathan, Timothy without Lois and Eunice, Apollos without Priscilla and Aquila.

Do you have a Jonathan in your life? A friend who stands by you, supports and encourages you, challenges you when you need to hear it and "strengthens your hand in God"? Are you anybody's David?

Do you have a Mordecai or a Deborah? They're the people who've invested in our lives with encouragement and support. They both challenge and inspire us, watch and pray for us. They have opened doors for us to walk through. They have given us opportunities in spite of other people's questions and our own inexperience and lack of confidence, and give us room to fail, learn and grow.

Sadly, this is an idyllic picture for far too many of us. Many female leaders long for sisters in leadership who can identify with their journey, but live with isolation. We search for accessible role models, longing for mentors who will train us up and guide our path, but we step out alone. We often surmise that such circumstances have strengthened our dependence on God, and we've learned valuable lessons in a wilderness. What we don't often admit quite as readily is that the isolation has sometimes wounded us, that the loneliness has sometimes weakened and maimed us. We've found it harder to stand firm against temptation and testing. We've not felt strong enough for greater risks or responsibilities because it's too much to take on alone. This chapter explores some ways to engage with other female leaders, so we can fan into flame the gifts that the Lord has poured out on us so richly, and passionately pursue the life he's got for us. We'll start with a particular pattern that is unfortunately rather a common experience in women's leadership, and a pattern we need to avoid in order to realize our potential: competitive relationships.

STILETTOS AT THREE O'CLOCK

Daytime TV talk shows remain something of an occasional guilty pleasure for me, but on this particular afternoon it was essential viewing. After all, it was a TV world exclusive, an interview that had needed to happen for over a decade. It was actually more intimate than an interview, in its own daytime TV kind of way, with no studio audience to cheer or clap: this was a conversation, and the cameras rolled. Finally, these two beautiful successful women who had been locked in a feud for over a decade were face to face. It was time for Tyra Banks and Naomi Campbell to talk it through, and kiss and make up.

Now obviously since this was Tyra's TV show and Naomi was promoting her perfume, I didn't expect a complete exposé, but as I'd followed their careers for years, I was committed. The interview itself was pretty TV ordinary: tears, hugs and a runway walk-off where the supermodels imitated one another's walks. A reconciliation made in TV heaven. Still, aside from the expected celebrity drama, aspects of the interview fascinated me. Both models spoke of how they'd been plagued by their own insecurity. When they started modeling, successful black models were rare, so others constantly compared them to and pitted them against one another. Although they look very different, it was made abundantly clear to them in various ways that there was only room for one black supermodel. Naomi had broken through first, so when Tyra arrived on the scene it was assumed that she was there to replace Naomi. Any hopes of fun, friendship or sisterhood were quickly buried under the reality that only one of them could dominate high fashion. Well, they both intended to succeed . . . and so the rivalry began.

Complicated competitive relationships among women are not limited to the catwalks and TV shows. A number of women I spoke to (from different countries and across a range of professions) noted how strained relationships with other female leaders had been.

Suzie Brock leads Wave of Life Ministries with her husband, Tom. They've spent the last thirty years traveling the world, training and mentoring leaders, serving and planting churches. Suzie observes: "Women leaders are naturally plagued by insecurity. Everything in society touts an image of perfect that none of us can be because we don't come with airbrushes to correct us. So we feel unworthy, and when we get with other women, we feel worse!"

> **Q. Are you locked into any competitive relationships with other female leaders in your field?**

We'll know if the presence of other female leaders makes us feel threatened. We compare our gifts and abilities, our talents. We'll observe their popularity and opportunities, their Facebook friends, and Twitter following. And perhaps we'll notice their age, their shape and their style. Whatever we notice, we'll know if we're competing even if we're unprepared to admit it. Because eventually, we'll feel it. In that slight discomfort that catches us off guard when we see her at work. Or the way we're a nanosecond late with our endorsement when someone else enthuses about her. The person talking might not even notice the way we stiffened slightly; we've worked to mask these feelings, because it's not something we're proud of. But we feel it. It's in the way we're suddenly motivated to work and push ourselves harder, or the way we inexplicably disengage from our responsibilities because we find it hard not to be number one. Sometimes this woman is a colleague we see occasionally, but sometimes she's a friend of ours, and a friendship under strain.

The writer of Proverbs observed that

A heart at peace gives life to the body,
   but envy rots the bones. (Proverbs 14:30)

We're blasted by anger and swamped by rage,
   but who can survive jealousy? (Proverbs 27:4 *The Message*)

Envy has a damaging effect on the person we are designed to be. It's hard to embrace the life and future God has for us when we are constantly wanting someone else's. And so we're worn down, our relationship with God is worn down, because we not embracing the *ezer* identity we've been given.

And jealousy? I'm always blown away by that verse—who can *survive* jealousy? Another translation says, "Who can stand before jealousy?" (TNIV). It humbles me because it's a reminder that, no matter how internal these attitudes are, they have an external impact. A relationship that could have been a source of encouragement and empowering can barely breathe after jealousy, corrosive like acid, has burned its way through it. Sometimes it seems there is no way back for the relationship. It's been devastating on occasion when I've experienced someone else's jealousy. But has that stopped me behaving in the same way? Of course not! If only.

A number of years ago I used to sing backup vocals, and led a worship team. If, when at an event, I heard another singer deliver a

riff or hit a note in a way that intimidated me I'd go home and practice it. I'd tell myself that I was developing ideas and skills, but
frankly I was never that disciplined! There was a motive behind it.
In "conquering" the riff, I was somehow keeping up with the other
worship leader. Maybe I was even better than she was—that's what I
was aiming for. In my heart I couldn't enjoy someone else's gifts
because I felt they were a threat to my own. Unfortunately for me,
there were lots of amazing singers around! Finally, after a lot of prac-
ticing at home (my poor neighbors!), I realized that I couldn't hope
to keep up, let alone "win." I also realized that I'd become incredibly
judgmental, and not surprisingly I was as insecure as ever! It was
time to get on my knees and confess my sin to God. I spent some
time, a lot of time, surrendering my attitudes and insecurities to
God. During that time of repentance, I sensed the Holy Spirit nudge
me to pray for blessings and opportunities for the women I was jealous of. Regularly. At first it was galling, if I'm honest; I felt as though
God was on their side (still competing, even in prayer!) and that I
was forgotten. It felt as though I was praying for success for them that
should have been mine. But God in his infinite patience and mercy
broke down the jealousy in my heart through those prayers. He
peeled off yet another layer of the insecurity that had enabled jealousy to have such a hold in the first place. He changed my heart,
and in time I had a completely different approach to the singers I
came across. I learned to make a habit of encouraging singers, until
it became natural to me. It was humbling, and healing at the same
time, that I should gain freedom out of this. And potential for
friendships too. I didn't deserve this. Have I ever felt jealous again?
Totally, but I'm more aware of my weaknesses now, so I've learned
to be more honest with myself and not let these things linger. I'm
aware that I'm quite naturally a competitive person, and I like to
push myself forward. That's one thing when I'm running and I want
to clock a faster time or a longer distance; it's another thing entirely
when I'm dealing with people.

> Q. What will you do with the competitive relationships, envy and jealousy in your life?

There's another dynamic that can emerge in some leadership teams that might also lead to competitive relationships. Sometimes, when a women leads, she has her job but then there is her role. It's as though her role is to be *the woman*. She's become the pioneer, the rare one who leapt over the brick wall, shattered the glass ceiling and navigated the labyrinth of choices and decisions to get where she is.[1] And because she's the woman on the team, she is to some degree incomparable. She has risen to the top, and that's significant because only one woman, it seems, is allowed at the top at any one time. (Remember the black supermodels?)

Then another woman joins the leadership team. It's exciting; finally a sister! We know we need more women in the upper echelons of church, business, the community, and so potentially here is someone who speaks the same language, who identifies with our journey. Finally, the chance to build a support network, to effect positive change. Isn't it? Yes, it is, but it can also be complicated. Who is this woman and what's her role? Is she *the woman* now? Has she arrived to take my place? Is there room for not just *a* woman at the top but *women* at the top? Did this new woman pay the price I paid, endure the misunderstandings, put in the hours? Or often behind that question—does it mean I am not enough? That she is better than me? More attractive, more competent, and so, more valuable?

Suzie recalled her own experience when she started out in ministry. "The women in the community avoided me for years, perhaps out of jealousy, fear and competition. And I was young and inexperienced, I really needed their support and guidance. But there was not a lot of coming to my aid, no support. It was lonely."

As a result Suzie made a decision over the years to act differently, even if it cost her emotionally at times.

When new women come through into positions of leadership—there's insecurity. So I have to forget again about me. I make an effort to get to know them, look out for them, serve them and bless them. I remember I can't be anyone else, but I can be me. It's OK, I have what I have, and that's Christ in me, the hope of glory. Why do I have to be the brightest star in the group? It was only ever about him, only about him.

The saddest thing about the dynamics I've described or other situations where competitive relationships arise is that this is nothing like the life God has for us. We are missing out on so much!

As the Teacher of Ecclesiastes writes,

Two are better than one,
  because they have a good return for their labor:
If they fall down,
  they can help each other up.
But pity those who fall
  and have no one to help them up! (Ecclesiastes 4:9-10 TNIV)

Together we can process the opportunities of leadership; we can help one another succeed. We can support one another when challenges knock us down. Like the biblical heroes who have gone ahead of us, we can release one another into who God created us to be. What would we change in the world around us if we won this battle inside ourselves? If we could serve, support and encourage each of the women leaders we know—what difference would it make?

I want to issue a challenge to every influential woman reading this book; whether you're a mother, an entrepreneur, a teacher, a church leader—make every effort in the next few months to make friends with the women leaders around you. If you already know them well, reach beyond your immediate network and make a new friend. I'm not saying ignore the women who aren't in leadership; that's equally counterproductive! But for the purposes of this particular conversation, I'm urging us to take the time to invest in building networks of relationships with other female leaders. Let's intentionally adopt the opposite attitude. They may be thinner than you, have a more celebrated voice than you; they may earn more than you. Be a friend anyway! They may have husbands while you're single. They may have shiny, perfect children. They may have more influence. But you know what? Do it anyway. Do it for them, because everyone needs a friend. Do it for yourself, because that "everyone" includes you. Rather than all struggling alone with loneliness and misunderstanding, weakened by our efforts, can we humble ourselves and seek to affirm and learn from one another? Perhaps I am being idealistic; we're all human, after all, and complications always come our way. But insecurity strangles the life out of us when it dictates our relationships. It wreaks havoc with our capacity to lead. Healthy friendships with other female leaders are something that we should fight for and work toward.

Paul went public with the broken relationship between two of his team in Philippi, pleading in his letter to the Philippians for Euodia and Syntyche to be reconciled, even enlisting Syzygus's help. Are you in a similar position, where a relationship with a fellow leader has broken down and is now affecting the community? If so, I'd encourage you to adopt the principles Jesus outlines in Matthew 18 as your modus operandi. Jesus states unequivocally that when someone sins against us *we need to address the person directly involved with a view to reconciliation.* If that is not working, then we bring in a third party, someone who has witnessed what has taken place. Then, and only after these two stages, does it become a matter for the wider church. Take your colleague out for a coffee, to a neutral venue, and work hard toward healing the relationship.

Mary and Elizabeth demonstrate a wonderful alternative of women working alongside one another in unity. Elizabeth was married to Zechariah the priest and so was a respected member of the community. Her pregnancy was a God-given miracle. In contrast Mary was a mere teenager, living a miracle that was shrouded in suspicion and local gossip. It must have been a lonely place to be. These distant relatives are thrown closer together as they support one another through this stage of their lives. Elizabeth celebrates Mary's faith and what God is doing in Mary's life, not comparing children or circumstances.

> In a loud voice she exclaimed: "Blessed are you among women, and blessed is the child you will bear! But why am I so favored, that the mother of my Lord should come to me? As soon as the sound of your greeting reached my ears, the baby in my womb leaped for joy. Blessed is she who has believed that what the Lord has said to her will be accomplished!" (Luke 1:42-45 NIV 1984)

Mary responds with an incredible paean of worship, and the women spend three hidden months together. Mary and Elizabeth's relationship brings a number of questions and reflections to mind.

> Q. Are we humble and secure enough to celebrate the amazing things happening in another woman's life? Even if her gifts are greater than our own? Even if she seems to get her opportunities more quickly than we do?
>
> Are we spending time in worship and prayer with other women? Do you ever retreat with the women in your life?

I'm aware that some of us have found the competitive relationships with other women incredibly damaging. We've pulled away from close relationships with colleagues now, certain that that is the only way to protect ourselves. Still, God longs for more than self-protective mechanisms for our wounds. He sent his Son to bring forgiveness, healing, redemption, reconciliation. And new beginnings. There's more for each of us than isolation from risks and relationship. What would it look like in your life if God could bring restoration to you in this area?

There is power and refreshment when we get together with other female leaders. It can be a balm to the loneliness that limits us, a place for accountability and encouragement when dealing with HALT, a change to dream and strategize, one *ezer* to another. We need to seek out networks and retreats for female leaders where we too can nurture, protect and cherish the great things the Lord is bringing about in our lives. And if we can't find any within our reach, do we need to prayerfully consider starting them?

FEMALE MENTORS

Have you struggled to find a mentor? Debs, a church leader, did:

> When I started in the workplace as a manager they were making major shifts in women in leadership. It took my denomination another decade before they started acknowledging women in leadership . . . and making a similar shift. So my main role models for ministry have been guys and they have done a fantastic job, because they've taught me brilliant stuff. But the reality is, who are the women ahead of me? Where are they?

Suzie reflected that one of the great sadnesses of her years in ministry was that she could count on the fingers of one hand the women who had come alongside her and spoken into her life. The sense of competition and insecurity got in the way of mentoring opportunities. Danielle Strickland observes an "orphan syndrome" among female leaders, stating that "women who have 'made it' without good mentors don't know how to mentor, release, and celebrate other women."[2] Perhaps they lack the tools or the time to make it possible, or think their own isolated experiences are inevitable for every woman who wants to lead.

Another observation is that there simply are not enough female leaders to go around. Despite the radical empowering of women that we saw in the New Testament church that modeled the value of women to the surrounding culture, it seems over time that we've gone backward in some areas. Perhaps we lost hundreds of influential forerunners to the limitations imposed by church and culture over the years. As a result, it seems that as we take hold of the twenty-first century a generation of young Christian women, passionate to step into God's calling on their lives, remains at an impasse. They want the tools, the wisdom and the insights they need to make an impact in their career, church or community, but remain uncertain of whom to turn to.

I believe that there are some ways to move forward, but it will require persistence and proactivity on our parts. Here are a few suggestions; see what you think.

First, it's obvious but *we need to pray.* Pray for the investment you need. Your call to leadership is not an accident, nor is it a concession because there are no guys available. God designed you and your gifts, he called you by name and he wants you to fulfill your calling. So seek him for what and who you need. Sometimes you'll find your answers in Scripture and in your prayer times; he'll mentor you directly. Sometimes he'll provide in the form of other people. But pray.

Next, please *don't wait to be chosen; be proactive.* If you want to buy a pair of shoes, you don't sit down waiting for them to turn up on your doorstep. You get out and look for them, explore your options, select what you need. Be practical about this and explore what is out there.

Debs suggested: "If you don't see many female leaders in the church, look for some good female Christian leaders in the workplace to mentor you. You'll find more there because the glass ceiling has been broken down a bit more and women have had more time and opportunity to take on a wider range of leadership roles."

Be aware that the best mentor for you may not come in the package you expect. Sometimes when we look for a mentor we look for someone like us, doing exactly what we're called to do. In addition we want someone who can identify with our lives in every way, who understands our every quality and quirk, a mother type with killer leadership skills and a bit of therapy thrown in. It's an understandable desire, but it might also be a romantic ideal and frankly a luxury. Most importantly, it might not be the person you actually need. If you need

professional counseling for some issues in your life or someone to pray
with you and minister to you, go for it and let the Lord use these resources to bring you to wholeness and freedom in him. A mentor,
however, has a broader role, an equipping role. They encourage you
and challenge you to be all that the Lord has called you to be.

I've had a number of mentors over the years, male and female (more
on the male mentor thing later). One of my favorite mentors, Sally,
who is now a great friend of mine, couldn't have had a life more different from mine. We have different colored skin, and she often has
shocking taste in music. She was at home bringing up three fabulous
children; I was single, leading missional communities and speaking at
conferences. But she was exactly who I needed. Sally understood leadership, and she knew how to walk with God as a secure woman. I
learned—still learn—lots from her life. I would have missed so much,
and my ministry and calling would have been profoundly lacking, if
I'd decided she had nothing to offer because our lives looked different.

So take another look around at the women in your community.
Ask yourself: are you sure there is no one there who can invest in
you? Sometimes you may find yourself in a mentoring relationship
for a while, but if that's not possible there's still room for *the mentoring
moment*. Look again at the women in your community that you ad-
mire and respect—even perhaps those you haven't until this point,
but really you should! Can you go out for a coffee, grab lunch—you
pay—and ask them a few questions about life? If that doesn't work
out, keep looking! One leader I spoke to went so far as to search out
a female spiritual director, in this instance a nun. The spiritual director was a great place for accountability and theological reflection,
often with a distinctly feminine perspective.

DISCOVER SOME CHRISTIAN HEROES

In addition to the biblical characters we've already looked at, Christian women throughout history have given us a great example of
what it looks like to pursue God's call on our lives. If you're passion-

ate about the mission field, look at the lives of women like Jackie Pullinger, Heidi Baker, Mary Slessor. If you have a passion for social justice and mission, look at Elizabeth Fry and Catherine Booth (and if you're a teenager, wondering if this applies to you, look out for Evangeline Booth). If you are a worship leader, look into the life of hymn-writer Fanny Crosby. There are many more women, from the seventh-century nun Hilda of Whitby, who founded monasteries and was sought out by royalty for her wisdom, through to Sojourner Truth, a nineteenth-century African American woman who, after being emancipated from slavery, preached the gospel around the United States and actively campaigned on behalf of the poor, for women's rights and for the abolition of slavery. What might you learn from their experiences?

Huddle. While one-to-one mentoring may feel ideal, I think one of the best ways we can grow is when we are mentored in a group setting. It may not be perceived as quite as intimate as one-to-one conversations, but it encourages accountability and provides leadership training—and a lot more women get mentored. The best example we can find of this in Scripture is when we look at Jesus' relationship with his disciples. Most of Jesus' personal investment in his disciples was while all of them, or a good number of them, were present.

My first experience of being mentored in a group was in Sheffield a number of years ago at my local church, where our vicar developed a model described as a "huddle" as a vehicle for intentional leadership development. The junior leaders on the staff team, a group of eight, met for an hour or so on a weekly basis. Using a list of simple but direct questions, we reflected on what God was saying about our character or about our skills.[3] The huddle leader would facilitate the discussions, but everyone made a contribution to the group. The huddle was not just a support group for leaders (it was often quite challenging!), but eventually each leader within the huddle gathered another group of people into a huddle to invest in. And then, even further down the line, those huddle members would look to gather yet more people to invest in. In the years that followed we saw many leaders equipped and ready to respond to God's call, be it to church, home or workplace, and an ongoing commitment to continue to raise up more influential men and women.

We're well aware of the lack of mentors for female leaders. As we address the problem, could God also be calling us to be part of the solution? We may not be able to change what we've lacked, but can we prevent the next generation of leaders from experiencing the same thing? Can you mentor someone? They might only be two steps behind you in life and work, but it makes a difference.

We need to find as many ways as possible to continually raise up influential women who in turn will raise up other leaders. Today, huddles are the primary way I coach and mentor leaders, male or female. It's exciting, and it's a privilege to see God raise up a generation of leaders in every sphere of life. It's also a context for me to listen, learn and grow. There is something special in discovering how others have lived this life, walked this walk. I don't ever want to get tired of learning from anyone I can, whether they're a biblical character, a Christian saint or another twenty-first-century woman like me.

Friends, mentors and healthy relationships are an integral part of leadership. Don't settle for isolation or competitive relationships. Find networks, join networks, create networks that bring you together with other leaders regularly. Be proactive in looking for mentoring opportunities. Do your part in raising up the next generation of female leaders to live out all they were called to be.

Reflections on Leadership

Naomi, a missionary in Mozambique:

Comparison and competition is the enemy! Spot this and go to Jesus and get healing when you see it in yourself.

Rich and Anna Robinson, leaders in St Thomas' Church, Sheffield:

- *Relationships—choose your friends wisely: it is vital to form safe, strong trusted counsel—peers and mentors. Identify and build relationships with people with whom you can be totally vulnerable as there is a deep level of trust.*

- *Relationships—recognize different levels of relationship: we need a range of relationships—those that are just fun and lighthearted/with accountability/totally transparent/peer/mentoring/leading—not judging any level of relationship as "better"—being objective about what the relationship is and what it isn't. Therefore, be realistic in your expectations—give, receive, be a peer, etc.*

- *Relationships—choose to allow people who are different to be close to you (e.g., different fivefold ministry, different personality types, different gifting) so that the rough edges are chipped off and you become more rounded and whole as a disciple, person and leader.*

Ali Herbert, leader of Girlzone, a women's ministry based at St. Mary's Bryanston Square, London:

1. *Get a great group of people around you. . . . And have some fun together. A small team of supportive people will encourage you when it's tough, inspire you to keep going, envision you with ideas beyond your own and keep you in touch with what people need. A supportive team is vital and life-giving. However, also be prepared to let people go. Your team will change over time for lots of reasons: as people go on to lead by themselves, as time or family needs press in, as they move on to a new vision, or literally just move to another (geographical) place. This can be painful to us sometimes as it's hard to lose great team members. The wise thing to do is let them go graciously—and bless them every time!*

2. *Pray with your team. . . . And don't just pray about your event or organization. Pray for each other's lives—pray for your needs, thank*

God for your answers to prayer, pray for your families, your workplace, your relationships. Your team will also be praying for you—it's a win-win situation. If you pray together and know your team authentically, it makes it so much easier to trust them to step out within your vision—and then see them go on to step out into their own vision. And that way, God's kingdom grows!

3. *Do something that energizes you. . . . And brings life to you. It's very hard to lead if you don't have a vision and a desire. We all find our passion waning at times, but I'd encourage you to do whatever you need to do to get the passion back. If we're not excited and motivated ourselves, then it's very hard to lead anyone else. Read a book, take time off, speak to someone who inspires you, go to a conference, go on a retreat or do a fast. Do whatever it takes, but just do it! God needs us to be passionate about what he's calling us to do.*

Gareth Robinson, church leader and worship leader:

You can't do it all yourself: give it away. Leadership is about inspiring, influencing and releasing other people—those who are following—to help them be the best they can be, creating space for them to succeed. That's servant leadership.

Lizzy Robinson, church leader and mother of three:

Leadership is about influencing others, not just public speaking. A public speaker might not influence anyone. So disciple people regardless of the platform; cheerlead them; empower and encourage them regardless of the personal cost—they may be better than you at some things which will touch your insecurities, but do it anyway. It's for God's glory, after all.

Navigating a Man's World

*In the beginning God made men and women. Both were equally an
expression of his image, character and love. Men and women were
commissioned together for both child rearing and ruling. Then the
fall happened and what was meant to be together got broken.
The world has been crying ever since.*

DAVID WESTLAKE, "WHY GENDER
EQUALITY MATTERS"

*Nowhere does God shine more brightly than when men
and women join in serving him together. This vital connection
between men and women enriches every aspect of life.*

CAROLYN CUSTIS JAMES, *LOST WOMEN OF THE BIBLE*

MEN ARE FANTASTIC! I'm very happily married to one; I'm a
younger sister to some fantastic ones, an aunt to some fine young
ones. I work with some great men and have done so for many years.
True, like many of us I've been wounded by a few men in my past,
but the One who saved my soul has redeemed me, brought healing
and restoration where needed, and forgiven me for those times when
I've done the wounding with the men in my life. But for all these
relationships, the good, the bad and the pretty amazing (hubby), I've

still had to learn to navigate my way as a leader in environments that
are predominantly male. I'm still learning, in fact. I've had to learn
what professional relationships with men might look like, particularly when I am the only woman in the room. I've needed to observe
how men talk and connect, discover what they value and what they
expect in a working environment. I've needed to work out how they
network, how they make friends. And then I've needed to work out
how I'm understood and perceived, how I communicate, how I network in that world, how I express expectations, emotion, opinion.
You see, my brothers already know me; they've seen me grow,
they've been a huge influence in my life, they understand me. But
this is a different world, and somehow I've got to navigate it respecting that there are differences between the genders while not making
sweeping generalizations about men—or women, for that matter.
No wonder it gets confusing sometimes!

How do we navigate our way as leaders in predominantly male
environments? Some of our paths don't cross into that world, while
for others it's our daily reality. This chapter draws on different leaders' experiences and offers a few suggestions for your journey.

WHAT'S YOUR FILTER?

Men are everywhere (I didn't think so when I was single, but hey);
we all relate to male relatives and friends on a daily basis. Spend some
time reflecting on your existing relationships with men in your family and friendship group. It's worth reviewing the nature of your
working relationships with men, whether it's your boss, those on
your team, your mentor, to make sure your expectations of them are
not projections of your significant male relationships, past or present.
Even when your environment is described as "one big happy family," there are still dynamics to consider. Can you treat your boss like
your big brother? And should you?

If your relationships with men have been difficult or painful, observe how that carries over into your professional life. Are you distant?

Suspicious, oversensitive, afraid? Do you only know how to relate to men in a sexual way? Has your personal history created a void, and as a result you crave male affirmation or attention? Have you experienced significant pain or neglect, violence or abuse in your relationships with men in the past and know that it casts a shadow over your life today? Before you even look at practical details on how to work with the men in your church, office or community, take some time to look at the filters that shape your perspective on men, and consider the best way to work through anything that comes to light.

Kate Smith, who leads a church with her husband in North Carolina, says:

> I think men and women need to recognize that they play out all their unhealed issues with Mom and Dad and family members in a church leadership team. So there can be anger, competition, judgments, feelings of being left out, of embarrassment, etc. We have noticed that the more we take responsibility for working out our own healing, then the less we see the sowing and reaping of judgments and expectations in other relationships. I find that I don't get as riled or angry about the male–female division as I used to because I am asking God to heal the root of pain in my own heart and expose any unforgiveness I maybe holding toward men who have been in my life who may have hurt me.

Do you need a new filter? What will you do to change it?

ARE WE DIFFERENT?

Are men and women different? If so, how do these differences affect the area of leadership and influence? Do men lead differently from women? Is there such a thing as masculine leadership and feminine leadership?

In her book *Play Like a Man, Win Like a Woman*, former media executive and leadership coach Gail Evans argues that women bring a more holistic view to the world of work, with more consideration for family obligations and a greater desire for strong relationships and personal fulfillment within the workplace. In contrast, she observes that men are more focused on the task at hand and place a higher value on rewards such as money, power and prestige.[1]

What do you think? We walk along this funny tightrope of trying to grasp a healthy understanding of our differences in leadership style and communication, while aiming to avoid the stereotypical assumptions of "Men are like this . . . while women are like that." In addition some of our definitions falter in multicultural settings, because cultures understand leadership and gender in different ways.

Leadership experts also note that the way men and women are brought up and socially conditioned plays a role in our differences: "From early childhood, girls are taught that their well-being and ultimate success is contingent upon acting in certain stereotypical ways, such as being polite, soft-spoken, compliant, and relationship-oriented. Throughout their lifetimes, this is reinforced through media, family and social messages."[2]

In contrast, they argue, boys are raised in a way that encourages competition and giving everything to winning: "From early childhood on, boys and girls play with different sets of rules. And because men created the rules in the game of business, and because women are only now trying to be effective competitors, we will prosper only when we are familiar with those rules."[3]

Broadly speaking, the difference we see in male and female approaches to leadership has the potential to be both exciting and confusing! It's exciting because a holistic emphasis that many women bring to the world of work can enrich the workplace and benefit everyone. The *ezer* is needed here! But if, as suggested, women are often conditioned to behave in particular ways, to embrace particular stereotypes, to be compliant, polite and not rock the boat, then it gets confusing. It's confusing because while it's essential that we develop excellent social skills, sometimes the *ezer* is called to challenge and confront the status quo. Sometimes God calls her to lead in dynamic ways, to speak out boldly and be an activist for change. How would Deborah or Priscilla have fit into this worldview? Would they have been seen as domineering? Aggressive or unfeminine, perhaps? Or would who they were help us define the breadth of what feminine looks like?

It's also confusing because, if men and women do play by different "rules" and women operate in predominantly male contexts, how do we thrive and grow into the leaders God has called us to be? In order to navigate our working environment, we'll need to be aware of the culture (and sometimes it's the hidden messages and expectations) of our working world. It's not always straightforward, as Kate Smith explains:

> Working with men has seen a few challenges for me over the last few years. It is often said that if a man is being assertive then he is a champion leader. If a woman is assertive she is considered pushy. As women we have to learn to grow in the confidence of God's calling in our life so that we learn to speak wisely and not respond in hurt or offence to men in our team. I have also encountered many cross-cultural differences working in a multicultural team. What is said in one context does not mean the same in another context. I have had to learn to forgive and ask for forgiveness for times I've taken offence or others have been offended by me, sometimes unknowingly. It is a fine line to walk but all can be conquered with the wisdom and grace of God. Wisdom is referred to in the Bible as female, and I think God knew that his daughters would need bucketloads to walk with our heads held up high in a man's world!

LEADERSHIP AND INFLUENCE:
IS IT A MAN'S WORLD?

In *Through the Labyrinth: The Truth About How Women Become Leaders*, Professors Alice H. Eagly and Linda L. Carli note:

Most leaders are men. Predictably, people think about leadership mainly in masculine terms. These mental associations about leadership not only shape stereotypes about leaders but also influence organizational norms and practices. . . . Over time organizational leadership inevitably has come to embody the preferences, lifestyles and responsibilities of the men who usually have held these leadership roles.[4]

In a culture that is simply not used to women leaders, women can be accidentally overlooked when we don't understand the implications of their lives outside their job are misunderstood. For example, leadership experts observe that male progression in leadership is generally much more lineal than for women. The seasons of their life may change—relationships, marriage, children—but they are able to retain their commitment and pace at work because of their support system at home, where their spouse takes on most of the domestic responsibilities. In both the workplace and the church, longer hours and the extra mile are not just endorsed; they are generally expected and seen as a mark of commitment and potential. The people who can step up to the plate like this are the ones to watch. These are the leaders of the future and should be invested in accordingly. However, for a woman, a new season of life means that her leadership path looks very different. A serious relationship, marriage, the birth of a child, more children or the needs of an aging parent can drastically redefine her life and the shape of her career. Extended periods away from work due to maternity leave can result in a crisis of confidence. A commitment to monitor the needs of family, sick children, school work, transportation to activities, means she has a number of priorities that can affect her job at any time. If the understanding of leadership embodies "the preferences, lifestyles and responsibilities of . . . men," it potentially presents a problem for this female leader. Thanks to her range of priorities, she may not be able to invest the extra hours, go the extra mile. Does it mean she is not as focused or committed as the men around her, and shouldn't be invested in? Does her life suggest that she does not have what it takes to step up to the next level of influence? The problem is, the culture may not understand that "what it takes" may not actually be about attitude or focus, but a support structure at home that frees you of any other demands on your time, energy and life.

HOW CAN YOU NAVIGATE YOUR WAY THROUGH?

> Each organization has its own structure—regular and predictable patterns of behaviour—and its own culture—shared beliefs, values, symbols and goals. Leadership is an important part of this social structure and culture.[5]

Is there a way to navigate the culture of your working world? We're not going to be able to change a culture overnight, but here are some suggestions to help you navigate the world you lead in.

Spend a week observing your working environment. Watch how people relate with one another. Observe working relationships between men, between women and between men and women. Pay close attention to the relationships that work well! Observe how people thrive in that environment, socially and professionally. Pay attention in meetings; observe the preferred forms of communication, in emails, phone calls, face to face. Are there unspoken rules that everyone knows must comply with? Then look at how your behavior compares with what you observe. See if your observations provide any insights into how to grow professionally or suggest any skills worth developing in order to help you thrive. Do you need to work on your communication? Do you need to present yourself differently, build relationships differently? It would be a shame (for both your workplace and you) if you missed out on realizing your God-given leadership potential simply because it was lost in miscommunication or missed relational opportunities.[6]

LEARNING TO NETWORK

One of the tools available to help us navigate a predominantly male context is networking. Sharon McQueary, an associate pastor in Ohio, gave this as her first tip for female leaders:

> Network! I failed to do this for many years in ministry. I had the false mentality that if God wanted it to happen, it would. I didn't want to seem too pushy as a woman in leadership. I didn't want anyone to think that I had worked my way up with little integrity. Really, I avoided the idea that I was entering into a career. However, I learned that men are networking. They are taking names and making connections with their careers in mind. We as women have been called to a career in ministry. It is our life and well-being and we have to network.

Perhaps to some of us the idea of networking seems a bit pretentious or presumptuous, as if we're schmoozing. It might even feel cold and ambitious that we're using people to get where we want to be, or the perhaps the idea of proactively building professional relationships seems strange. Networking can be challenging in a predominantly male environment. It might revolve around traditionally male sports like golf that you might not play; you might feel uncomfortable or unable (or uninvited) to join in the guys' football game. Some of us walk away from networking opportunities because afterhours drinks means longer hours at work, when we have children's homework and domestic chores to consider. In addition, conversations can be challenging—I recall one particular night out at a retreat with thirteen male leaders, when the conversation revolved around vasectomies for well over an hour. I didn't have much to contribute! It's understandable that we steer away from networking, but does it cost us opportunities? Not so much the opportunity to get ahead, but if God's called us to a position for such a time as this, there may be kingdom opportunities involved. There may be people we might lead to Christ, opportunities for positive influence.

How do we make a way through? If you know that networking is something you need to do more of, again, look at the people around you who are doing it well. If you can't adopt all their ideas, what ideas can you adapt? Lunch instead of after-hours drinks? Conversations about family or shared interests, or about projects you're working on, or ideas, or skills you have? "People bond through networks both within their organizations and beyond them. Good relationships make it possible to call on others for support, ranging from getting advice and information to setting up deals and transactions."[7]

Cathy Moore, a leadership coach and missional leader in Seattle who has experience in the corporate world and nonprofit organizations, offers a couple of networking suggestions:

> Never join in on the heavy banter, sexual joking or flirting. You may feel like one of the gang, but the potential for losing respect is high. Light banter is one thing, but never go toe to toe. If you open this doorway they will fall in and you'll end up the loser. Remember, it is okay to jokingly say, "Enough, boys!" My advice is, you don't know what light banter is until you have been around a while, and it changes even within a group depending on the setting or those present, so keep the lips closed and observe the women that are highly respected and the men that are highly respected and listened to (they are not necessarily the most liked) and emulate them while you find your way.
>
> Pay attention to your calendar when making appointments with men. Talk about learning the hard way! I invited a client out to lunch to network and develop a stronger working relationship. He was single and I, although engaged, did not have an engagement ring. I did not really check the date and made a lunch appointment. It was not until afterwards that I figured out why he was acting a little too odd and then upset when I mentioned my fiancé. I had invited him to lunch on February 14!

IT'S COMPLICATED

For all the navigating and culture-watching, sometimes it is just complicated.

Mary couldn't understand why, when she spoke up at the team meeting, her views were overlooked, but when a man said the same thing he was somehow heard and validated. Was it her communication style or was there more to it?

Becky worked hard on her management team. She excelled in everything she did, and companies that worked with her organization pointed it out regularly. Yet whenever a new and exciting opportunity arose, the project was given to someone less competent and less qualified than she was. Every time this was a man. Nothing had ever been explicitly said about how her boss viewed female leaders. But after watching this pattern for a number of years, she began to wonder.

Sarah wasn't sure if she was expected to laugh at sexist jokes, or smile sweetly at yet another patronizing remark. She wondered how she would navigate the old boys' club that surrounded her at work. Should she just toughen up? How many times would she have to fight back the tears? She knew it would only make things worse if she cried.

Beth and John worked as a team in ministry in clearly defined roles. Yet whenever a question was asked, John was automatically consulted, even about Beth's responsibilities. It was particularly upsetting when other members of staff did this.

Amanda wondered if she'd ever get her voice heard in the staff meeting. Surrounded by excited visionary men, as soon as she began talking they would cut across what she was saying and take it somewhere else. How would she regain their attention?

Nicole wasn't sure if she was feeling sensitive that day, but when the worship kicked off the team meeting all she could hear were male voices. Today it reminded her again that she was the only woman in the room.

How would you respond in any of these situations? Would you get angry, upset? Would you tell anyone?

A PROBLEM SHARED,
A RESPONSIBILITY HALVED

When our roles get complicated, it's important to be open about the differences and the difficulties women experience in leadership. We may already share this with other women, but do the men we work with know about it? We don't need to talk about it all the time, but they do need to know what it's like sometimes and how it affects us. Some things are said and done out of ignorance, and will be changed over time. We cannot expect to be automatically understood by the opposite sex, nor to automatically understand. Is it ever fair to expect someone who's never walked in your shoes to understand the difficulties on your path? A man couldn't automatically understand what sexism toward women feels like, or know the frustrations of the glass ceiling, but for healthy discussions with women he works with it's important that we hear from one another, learn from one another.

I'm privileged to work alongside some very strong men, who respect and listen to my perspective and my occasional frustrations. But for a long time I didn't talk about things I experienced, because I didn't want to make excuses, I didn't want to feel emotional, I didn't want to make a big deal of the gender thing (or also, in my case, the racial issues that crop up occasionally)—I just wanted to do a good job in spite of these things. Eventually I realized that this approach was a mistake. Not only because things I'd encountered would fester within me until I reached a boiling point, but also because the reason I lacked the support of my male colleagues was that they didn't know what was happening. I've since learned to share my experiences. Not just the big things, but I simply talk about what it's like sometimes. I need to be open about the vulnerability I sometimes feel as a woman in leadership in the church. I've also learned to be open to hear when I've misinterpreted a comment or a situation, and to listen to a male perspective on it. Most of all I know that, as part of a team, I don't go through anything alone. A problem shared is a responsibility halved. I don't have to fix everything that isn't working for the female leaders

I see around me. I am part of a team, so when something comes up we are all affected, and together we look for creative solutions. Share your stories even if it's stilted at first, even if it's hard work. Communication provides a context for understanding and awareness, and for getting the help you need to navigate the world you're in.

OTHER PEOPLE'S OBJECTIONS

What if someone (male or female) says I shouldn't be in leadership because I am a woman?

Anne Maclaurin, senior vicar of St. Barnabas, Cambridge, says,

My male mentors have been instrumental in dealing with other people's objections to my position in leadership. When I was about to start as a curate in a new church, I asked my mentor, "What do I do if people in my own congregation say that they don't agree with women in leadership?"

"Don't argue with it," he replied. "Ask your male leaders to go and have the conversation with them. They are coming to you concerning a decision that you didn't actually make! You were employed by someone and invited to take up that role. If someone else has a problem with it, encourage them to talk to the person who chose to employ you."

What should you do if your church has a specific position against women in leadership? Do you leave the church? Can you bring change from within a system, or will you just get so damaged in the process that it is simply not worth it? Opinions vary on this among the different leaders I spoke to. Some said there was little point in staying in a place that did not endorse your call, while others felt there was more of a journey involved in processing the church's stance.

Anne says:

I think you have to have the conversations with your leaders. Go with the biblical material, and ask them to read through it and work through it with you because you sense a call to leadership. If you do decide it's time to leave, do so in as positive a way as possible. Otherwise, people just pick up their toys and leave a place, forgetting that there are still relationships you have in the church to consider. If you are going to leave, leave well. Bless them and go.

MENTORING

In Esther's story we've seen the power of male/female mentoring. A number of us may find that the leaders ahead of us are male and that they become our role models, either from a distance as we watch and follow their careers or ministries or more directly, as mentors. It can be such a positive experience learning from someone so different from you, and can give insights on how to navigate areas often dominated by men. I've been so blessed by the male mentors I've had. They have trained me and skilled me and listened to me—and given me opportunities, sometimes their own opportunities, so that I could grow into who I was called to be. These mentors seemed to know ahead of time—something I've only recently understood—that in some fields women leaders need the men to open the door for them. Not because the women have been less able, but because the handles to some doors of opportunity have been on the other side of the door! And my mentors were committed to opening doors for *whoever* was called, male or female. So I was often part of small teams of men and women who accompanied my mentors on mission trips and conferences, or to the coffee shop for a discussion.

Some individuals greet the male/female mentoring idea with caution or fear. Too many leaders have fallen; too many people have abused power and influence in a relationship that seemed to begin innocuously. Is this asking for trouble? It's an understandable caution, but we have to pay close attention to the implications of our response.

In church settings, a number of women speak of a common scenario. They've watched their male peers on their teams receive lots of mentoring from their senior male leaders, and have received none themselves. They watch them go on trips and enjoy lunches and meetings. On one level they understand that this primarily reflects a desire to maintain healthy male-female boundaries. But when they see their male peers thrive in a mentoring relationship that they cannot have, it can be painful. Sometimes it breeds resentment as they watch their male peers enjoy new responsibilities and opportunities because mentoring has developed their leadership capacity. Confused, these women are uncertain whether this is because they themselves are not gifted or qualified for greater responsibility, or because they have never had a mentor to uncover and develop their gifting.

We don't want to be blasé about boundaries, but nor do we want to prevent the opportunity for a generation of Christian female leaders to be equipped and empowered for the church and for the workplace. It's absolutely tragic and fear-bound. I believe there are ways we can move forward on this, which may require creativity but are totally worth it. The huddle that I spoke of in the previous chapter is a great practical example.

We women also have our part to play in this. As a woman mentored by men, I was conscious of boundaries and decided in advance what my values and practices would be. I decided early on that if ever I was mentored by a married man, I would get to know his wife and family too. Not because I was trying to be a stalker, but because then it wasn't an exclusive relationship. The result has been incredible: it gave me two mentors at a time instead of one. In written communication I'd generally copy in the spouse or another leader, again to avoid being exclusive. On the occasions when my leaders were single, again my principle was simply not to develop a relationship that was so exclusive that boundary lines were crossed.

The rest, I think, is just about our own common sense and self-awareness. There's no need for late-night conversations or intimate dinners. If I was going through something especially personal, I would seek out a woman to process it with. And if I ever had a crush on someone inappropriate, I would walk away, so why would a mentor be different?

> **Q. How do you feel about being mentored by a man, and what values and practices would you want to put into place?**

INVENT YOUR OWN LEADERSHIP STYLE

Anne Maclaurin says:

> As a young commercial management trainee, I was trained by two men on the sales floor, both commercial managers. We worked with supervisors who are largely women. I noticed that the way the men got the staff team to do what they wanted/ needed to get done was by using a general chatty, flirtatious approach. The women loved it, because it was jovial and friendly. But it wasn't going to work for me! I was new, and again there hadn't been a woman on this side of management before; I needed to develop my own style. I decided to get to know the supervisors—to do it by showing that I could do a good job and be reliable, but also by getting to know them as people, asking after their families and their lives outside work. So instead of "Hey, you're looking gorgeous today, love, can you move that counter over there for me?" I asked about their journey into work, their families, and then the job at hand. I had to innovate my own different style so that I could establish good working relationships in that environment. I learned a lot from my leaders, but I needed to be me.

As leaders we'll continually grow, learn and mature. We'll develop skills and sharpen our talents. We'll use different leadership styles for different contexts. Sometimes we will need to be directive; at other times we will need to coach; sometimes we will need to hold someone's hand. When we look at the life of Jesus, we see that he adapted his leadership style according to the situation. But as you navigate this world, be yourself. Take up the tools you need to navigate your way through a predominately male context and fashion them so that they can work in your hands. Don't be embarrassed by your boldness, nor ashamed of your tenderness. God made you, so you are clearly good enough. Find your own voice, your own style, and lead as he leads you.

I'll leave the final thoughts with other leaders on the journey.

Reflections on Leadership

Annwen Stone, church leader, King's Centre, Sheffield:

When I first started in the team I am in now, my self-confidence was low. I had been out of the workplace and at home with children for seven years. I knew God had called me but somehow and somewhere I had lost my voice. I would hear discussions and decisions being made about the future of the church and find myself hiding and holding back because my opinion seemed so different to the men around the table and therefore, I deemed, "wrong." I am not someone who enjoys conflict and the thought of coming across as a bolshy feminist was not my bag, so I hid. As time went on (and frustration in me built) I discovered, with the use of resources like Myers-Briggs, that actually my viewpoint was exactly what was needed for the right balance of the team. That my intuitive and relational ability was what the team needed to help them make whole and good decisions. Accepting myself and letting go of the assumption that I'm wrong just because I might offer a different opinion has been so releasing. I have a voice again.

Sharon McQueary, associate pastor at Hope Community Church, Toledo, Ohio:

Find great supporters/encouragers!

Being a woman in ministry is often a lonely place. Find someone who can watch your back, who can be there to encourage and support you through the good, bad and the ugly of your life. Seek them out! Christian life was never meant to be done alone, and often when we step into leadership as women many things happen that cause us to feel as if we are standing on the center of a broken bridge, with our congregations on one side—who are often just oblivious—and the world of the male-dominated leadership on the other. Find both men and women on both sides of the bridge who support you and who you can depend on for encouragement.

Glenn Kahler, senior pastor, The Gathering Network, Kansas City:

Don't assume men understand the unique challenges and needs you have as a woman. So be willing to teach them how you are different. My wife and daughters have taught me many things, such as that getting into an elevator alone with a man is a very different experience for a woman than a man for safety issues—most men have no idea how women feel in these types of normal life events.

Don't try to be men. Be secure enough to be a woman.

Be secure enough to be a servant. Serving isn't a statement of role or value, or "below" any of us, because it is what Jesus did.

From my perspective, leadership and where you serve is primarily a "gift" issue, not a gender issue. Know that you have a unique and valuable perspective as a woman that is needed and makes the team stronger. You'll have greater influence if you "earn the right to be heard" beyond just being a woman.

Blakely Page, nutritionist and lay missional leader at The Gathering Network:

Be a student of those you lead with. Understand their passions, their personality and their giftings in order to serve and bless them by communication styles that offer them freedom and safety as difficult roads are navigated as a team. Learn, even through muddled mess-ups, how to communicate feelings, hurts and confusions in ways that include but are not driven only by emotion in timely ways that allow communication among leaders to remain open and flowing.

Kate Smith, who leads a church with her husband in North Carolina:

If we can aim to develop a culture of love and honor in our relationships and in our leadership teams, then the fruit of this will grow and blossom. If each of us can begin to prefer others above ourselves, then truly the kingdom of God will be revealed! I want to be a part of the solution of love and honor and learning to think like Jesus, who laid down his life as a servant of all.

For women leaders, the different stages and seasons of life can redefine what leadership looks like. We embrace certain limitations and discover new opportunities. Over the next few chapters, we'll look at some life lessons learned and tools discovered by different women in different seasons of life, which will hopefully give you some ideas and food for thought on your own journey!

Leadership in the Key of Life

We're here for a reason. I believe a bit of that reason is to throw little torches out to lead people through the dark.

WHOOPI GOLDBERG

Everyone has a transferable commodity-knowledge. Sharing your unique expertise and making introductions for someone creates a lasting legacy.

MARSHA BLACKBURN,
U.S. CONGRESSWOMAN, TENNESSEE

I'M LOOKING FORWARD TO THIS EVENING. The kids are tucked up in bed sweetly sleeping. My husband is watching football and will do so for hours. The evening is mine. I'm in the corner of a restaurant in a booth. It's public enough to feel the atmosphere in the room, private enough for intimate conversation. I'm almost embarrassed to say that I'm slightly giddy with excitement, but this is a special event. It's not every day I get to spend time, hours, an entire evening, with women like these.

I don't know how I guessed it, but I knew who would arrive first. It's Priscilla. She's walks with an understated elegance. Her style is not quite Lydia's purple chic, but simple and tailored. She seems quite tall at first, but I soon realize that it's more that she has presence;

Priscilla's radiant confidence makes her seem larger than life. But then Priscilla has lived a big life. I waste no time, and conversation overflows with stories from her pioneering missionary adventure, observations of the cultures she has visited and ministered in. Her mind is an incredible resource; she is sharp and engaging. And I notice a softness in her smile and her gaze when she mentions Aquila.

I don't know how much time has passed when Deborah arrives. She has a regal beauty, a face that reminds me of Toni Morrison. I see authority and strength in her poise; depth and maturity are in her eyes. The lines on her face and hands tell of a lifelong journey that I'm desperate to hear about. She tells me stories, stories of everyday situations, stories of everyday people who sought her out for advice and help. She tells stories of a covenant community who sometimes lost their way. And stories of battle and warfare. I'm transfixed.

We hear the final guest before we see her. She's chatting with the staff at the restaurant, laughing. She almost bounces toward the table and warmly greets everyone with hugs and a warm smile. She's carrying lots of bags and her phone keeps buzzing until she switches it off with an apologetic smile. I can see this is a woman who's hard to get annoyed with, and I don't even know why yet. She's attractive, seemingly ageless, vivacious and dynamic. She is what my American friends call "adorable." I'm already a little in awe of her. Where Priscilla informs me and Deborah inspires me, this woman, if I'm honest, totally intimidates me. She talks about property and investments in one sentence, then her humanitarian work, and finally is talking about her home and family! Wow! And she's clearly in great shape. I don't even know her name. But when I see a thick gold band on her wrist, I can't help but wonder if Wonder Woman really does exist, and if Mrs. Proverbs 31 is also known by that name.

As conversation flows, they graciously allow me to ask as many questions as I want. "Priscilla, what was it like to be more prominent than your husband back then? Did it create tensions between the two of you? Did people judge you or assume things about you?" I want to know too what it was like working alongside Paul, and how she responds to the various claims made in his name concerning women in leadership.

With Deborah I just want the wisdom. What did she learn about the human condition as she settled disputes over the years? How did she not get overwhelmed with everyone else's problems? And how did she know the answers? And I want to listen to what it was like to lead the people to war, to win a war and then craft a song.

With the Proverbs 31 woman (still not sure of her name, though for now still holding on to the Wonder-Woman theory) my questions are practical. "How did you do it? How did you know what to do?" She has a busy life, diverse priorities and interests. I'd love to learn how she made them run smoothly, how she knew how to live her God-given life in such a big way. I'd love to learn from them all about how they invested in their marriages and families. There's so much to ask, so much to learn, so much to know. I pull out my notebook to refer to my questions.

When I look up, the women have gone. Of course, they were never there. I'm still in a restaurant in a corner booth, public enough to soak up the atmosphere, private enough for intimate conversation. The kids are home asleep, my love is watching football, and I have a night to retreat, find some space, be with God. I still have so many questions on the "how" of life when you're in leadership. I look down and I see my Bible open at Proverbs 31 and bookmarks in Judges and Acts, and other books, Ruth, Esther, the Gospels, Romans. And while their names and stories jump off the pages, sometimes I long to see, really see, all the details of their lives too.

LEADING IN THE KEY OF LIFE

I wonder if you know where I'm coming from. Have you ever wanted to talk to someone about the details of life as a leader? Sometimes it's not so much the task or gifts that I want to process, it's how it fits with dating, getting married, having kids and living grown-up life. The details that you are left with when the words from the Lord have been received, when the promotion is secured, and now it's not a dream or vision, it's just real life. We know that life has different stages, each with opportunities, but also with limitations. Somehow we need to work out how to embrace and engage with our God-given calling and influence each stage of life we're in. Our calling can be shaped and expressed differently in different stages of life. So, for example, what could life look like for the single, influential woman? For the married, influential woman, the influential mother? Nonetheless, rather than be guided by our own personal or cultural assumptions, our challenge is to learn how to stay close to Jesus so that like him we can do only what we see the Father doing (John 5:19) in every season of our lives.

I've found it incredibly helpful to learn from other women further along on the journey and be reassured by them, guided, led. I've needed more than vision and inspiration: I've needed details, texture, something practical to work with. So while we don't have the details from our biblical (super) heroines, we still have each other. Perhaps we can show one another how we do it.

These next two chapters offer some stories and lessons learned in the trenches of leadership. They share how women have embraced the changing shape of their call and influence in different seasons of their lives, as single women, as married women and as mothers. There's opportunity for reflection, some questions to answer, and some creativity of your own to give birth to as you apply these lessons to your own world, as you lead in the key of life. Get yourself a corner booth, grab yourself a coffee, and spend some time with us. We'll start with a group who are particularly close to my heart, single women in leadership.

SINGLE LEADERS

Can single women influence the world around them for the kingdom in big, God-glorifying ways? Of course they can—and it's wonderful to see. They're content as single women, whether it's for a season or for life. Women like these are not defined by their marital status. They're living out the God adventure and don't need us to tell them by word or deed that they really cannot be leaders unless they have a man to complete them. We see in Acts in Paul's third missionary journey that he stayed in Caesarea at the house of Philip the Evangelist, who had four unmarried daughters who prophesied (Acts 21:9). Scholars note that these women were established as leaders in the Caesarean church, and that later early church leaders and Christian historians such Eusebius acknowledge this.[1] We see it in the lives of missionaries and Christian leaders throughout history

It's the story of many women leaders today too. So we don't need to limit our sisters with our cultural or preferred expectations, as happened to one friend:

> Marriage in certain streams of the Christian church seems to be an unhealthy obsession. In the church I worked for, I wasn't taken as seriously as my married male colleagues, and I was often told that I needed to be married and that I was wrong for not wanting to be. As a single woman who was happy being single, I was treated with suspicion and disregard. Even a male colleague told me once that there's no way they would have treated me as badly as they did were I married, nor, I suspect, were I a man. I was only a baby then, only in my mid-twenties, but even at that age being single was seen as weird in a culture where a lot of folk married as soon as they graduated from university. In the "real world," where I work now, I don't get any of that sort of nonsense going on. I'm one of the younger members of staff, some of whom are married or in relationships, some of whom aren't—but I am treated the same as others at my level.

THE SEASON OF MY DISCONTENT

Many women leaders understood the opportunities that singleness offered a long time before I did! As a single woman, I wrestled long

and hard with even *acknowledging* the season and the opportunities
the Lord had for me. As far as I was concerned, I wanted to be married and the leadership got in the way. Leadership was what I would
do until Mr. Right came along . . . then we'd lead together or I'd be
the great woman standing behind him, supporting him all the way.
Somehow I'd got it into my head that there were only two options,
marriage or leadership, and I couldn't have both.

Extended periods of singleness seemed to mean that the Lord had
made his decision! As a result I spent a lot of emotional energy wrestling with God's call on my life. There was a day when my pastor
offered me a promotion at work. I can recall his bemused face when
I responded, "You do know you're ruining my marriage prospects,
don't you?" Eventually I accepted the promotion, and the internal
wrestling that accompanied it.

I couldn't embrace the life I had because it wasn't the one I
wanted. So internally I was struggling and wrestling, which in
itself was draining. I cannot tell you how many times I prayed
about this, cried over this, or simply spent days, weeks, months
miserable about this. If there was any opportunity to embrace
that season, I wasn't looking at it. There were times my strength
and my faith waned. Then externally, I was working extra-long
hours to fill up my life so that I didn't have to think about it. And
if I wasn't working, I was thinking about work—planning, strate-
gizing, dreaming, stressing. I had no time for anything else, but I
didn't take any personal responsibility for the life I wanted and
didn't yet have. And I was slowly but certainly burning out. Remember HALT?

AN ADVENTURE WITH A GOOD GOD

A number of things gave me some much needed clarity. Daily heart-
burn for three months was a bit of an indicator that something was
wrong! Time spent with friends reminded me that I didn't do that
nearly enough. The loving concern in the voices of mentors couldn't

be ignored for ever. And a conversation in the pub with a fellow single sister articulated exactly what was going on.

"You look at your life as marriage or ministry. And right now God's given you these massive ministry opportunities. But you're reaching for something that is simply not happening yet. I don't feel he's saying it's one or the other. I think he's saying embrace what he's put in front of you and he'll take care of the rest."

So I did. I decided that I would see what life could be if I embraced being a leader as a single woman. I said yes to things I thought my hypothetical husband would do, and assumed that since the door had opened for me, it was well for me. I embraced my community, my single and married friends, realizing that when God said it wasn't good for humanity to be alone (Genesis 2:18) that included me and was about humanity's design for community, not purely marriage. So I made time for friends and family and time for myself, and I enjoyed it. Work was fantastic, but it would not be my life. My life would be my life, and I had to take some responsibility for that. I remember New Year's Day, arriving in Sydney airport and thinking just how great life was. I was young and single and free to be wherever the Lord placed me, and that didn't automatically mean loneliness and burnout. I had a greater capacity for certain roles; I could respond to challenges and opportunities that my married colleagues couldn't. I could study and train and travel with greater flexibility for extended periods of time. I was on an adventure with a good God.

CHALLENGES TO THE GOD ADVENTURE

Still, we know every adventure has its challenges, and this adventure is no exception! Single women face a number of challenges in the world of leadership.

For some, the issue is theological. When Jane was given a mentor during her ordination process, she was excited. But it was difficult to hear that, though he supported the ordination of women, he didn't believe that they should lead a church. And he reminded her regularly that he, as a man, was her spiritual authority.

For others, it's loneliness. One of my single missionary friends spoke about the loneliness of her calling, saying, "I love what I do—it's what I'm called to and I'm passionate about it. But sometimes you do wish you had someone there to talk with you, to be with you. To give you a hug, to stand with you and share." She said that, as a single woman, her relationships with the men she worked with were sometimes distant and awkward. "I understand that people want to have boundaries and I respect that. But it's hard when the men you work with—and their wives—view you as a sexual threat."

Isn't it a tragedy (and not a little insulting) when we isolate our sisters on account of our narrow views and insecurities?

Others have struggled to be taken seriously. Cassie, a youth worker, was about to take the youth group on a long trip using a fifteen-seater passenger van. A church elder called her and asked, "Have you driven one of these before?" "Yes, many times." "Well, tell me about the experience!" The conversation ended with the elder requesting that Cassie should phone him to tell him everyone had arrived back safely. "I felt as if I was about sixteen!" she laughed. Perhaps the elder was just being a bit paternal, supportive even. But Cassie couldn't help but wonder if her male counterparts would have received the same phone call.

When Susan dealt with conflict on her team, she found that they rarely responded. She later learned that her supervisors consistently went behind her back and talked directly with her team to deal with the same situation. "It completely undermined my position," she said. Her opinions and insights were generally ignored. When she shared her insights with a male colleague and he raised the exact same point in team meetings, her views were acknowledged and endorsed. The sad thing for her was that they were endorsed as her colleague's views and insights, not her own.

Q. What does it look like for you to embrace and engage with leadership and influence in this season of your life?

What are the opportunities?

What are your challenges?

Things to consider:

- Establish your boundaries. As a staff member of a team, your need for rest and relaxation is as valid as for those who are married, or with children. Are you working more hours than you should, or have you learned to set boundaries? This is easier in some professions than others!

- If you are working more hours than required, spend some time reflecting why.

- Everyone is designed for community. Are you part of a healthy faith community?

- Working relationships? Have you sought out relationships, networks, with those who understand the dynamics of your profession and can give you advice on how to live it out?

- Time for you. Are you taking time for yourself? Are you doing things you love and enjoy?

- Do you have a season of discontent? How do you feel about not being married? If singleness is a consistent ongoing struggle for you, how are you attending to that area of your life?

- Are you content as a single woman except for dealing with the people who keep harassing you about your marital status? It seems we often forget that singleness is as much a gift to the church and community as marriage is (I know I certainly did). Don't let anyone steal your contentment, but I'm sure you already know that well-meaning people will constantly question your marital status. If you're happy and you know it, come up with a sound bite! Sadly, you cannot stop everyone from asking questions, but can you find a reply that politely but firmly ends the conversation? How about these:

"I'm really happy with my life at the moment! How's yours?"

"So many men, so little time."[2] (Be warned: this line has been known to backfire!)

A quick word on leadership and dating: What if you're single to mingle? It's important that we remember that our leadership position is one area of our lives, not everything. It's probable you'll meet people you're attracted to in your working life. Consider the filters you use when assessing their compatibility! Sometimes we are in danger of judging compatibility with someone on account of their profession rather than their character, their bank balance rather than their walk with God. We might spend more time looking at their future calling and gifting than at how they treat us and relate to others. Spend some time considering what truly matters. And try not to take yourself too seriously. Some of us avoid relationships because we feel that our position of leadership is like living in a fishbowl and everybody is watching us, and it feels like pressure. Hate to say it, but really no one is that interested in our lives for that long! It's just another piece of news; there'll be another headline eventually.

ADVICE FROM THE SINGLE LADIES
FOR THE SINGLE LADIES

Don't listen to the lie of "I need a husband to do this."

Rest—that doesn't always mean time alone. Plan fun things or weekly "date nights" with friends. It's as important for you as it is for your married colleagues!

Holidays and retreats are important too. They are not an optional extra.

You need your tribe/family of people to be open with. Make an effort to be vulnerable (not needy), to share with them how you are really doing. Have people in your life who pray for you and love you for who you are and not what you do. Develop friendships where people know you and encourage you to be someone other than your job or ministry.

A Change in Season

Women can have it all, but not all at once.

MICHELE GUINNESS

FOR TEN YEARS, LEADERSHIP HAD pretty much been about me and the Lord. My gifts, vision, skills, opportunities, serving him. One glorious day, a rocking white dress and a honeymoon in Cuba later, and suddenly life was all about a brand new *us* with him! Obviously it wasn't exactly sudden, but marriage certainly changed our lives, and brought me a broader understanding of calling and what God's priorities look like. I knew I totally was in love with my man and excited to spend the rest of my life with him. But I was uncertain of what it would mean for me as a leader. It took some time to get my head around the way leadership and marriage flowed together. I was unsure of what I was supposed to be now. I'd invested my single years in leadership opportunities, and when I finally embraced them I enjoyed them! Did marriage mean that I needed to step down from leadership and become a different person? Sometimes I wrestled with the lingering insecurity that the same strength in leadership that was good when I was a single woman was now dominance and manipulation in marriage. I wondered if to take on a leadership role was somehow disrespectful to my husband and a sign of being a control freak! That's why I wanted an evening with Priscilla, with Deborah and with Mrs. Proverbs 31. Because they were healthy, strong married women, influential in their respective spheres, called and anointed by God.

I wasn't the only one who wondered. I've met many women who have shared the same concerns. They feel called to leadership, and their husband sees and endorses it too. There is grace and fruit in their public ministry, but they still wonder if they should be doing it. One woman once asked me if she should marry the man she was in love with because while she was an up-front leader in the church, he was only influential behind the scenes. Was it a bad sign? (I said no, it *wasn't* a bad sign. And for the record, we've totally overemphasized visible aspects of leadership and ministry in the church.) Ironically my good friend Alicia encountered a different cultural moment at the other end of the spectrum. Alicia knew she was called to be a pastor's wife. But sometimes people responded as though she had singlehandedly set women's freedoms back by a generation! Thankfully, Alicia knew her God and her call, so she would never waver for long. Here's her story.

> One Sunday night at youth group we had one of those "if you feel called to ministry, come to the altar" calls. I didn't go up, but I did ask to talk to my youth minister afterward. I told him that during the prayer time I felt that I wouldn't be a pastor (at least the ordained kind) but I felt that God was saying I would be a pastor's wife. I don't know if anyone had said that to him before; he didn't really say anything, no sense of direction, words of encouragement, nothing! I shared it with my mum, too. She gave me a strange look, as if to say, "Whatever." After I got those reactions from the adults I had confided in, I didn't tell many other people! While I obviously didn't screen every guy I dated to make sure they were going to be pastors, I knew it wasn't me just making it up. And then there was Greg.

(And yes, she is a pastor's wife. Greg and Alicia are currently planting a new church.)

The most helpful advice when we got married came from my church leader and his wife. They encouraged us to observe different models of marriage, and encouraged us to discover with the Lord the model he had for us, rather than feel there was one specific way we "ought" to be. They listed a number of couples leading within our church, observing how strong their marriages were and yet how different they were. In one couple the husband had a very prominent position while his wife contentedly held a supportive role. Another couple led together. Yet another saw the husband function in a supportive, sometimes invisible, role, while his wife was a recognized visible leader. It was releasing to know that one size didn't fit all when it came to leadership and a strong Christian marriage.

> Q. If you're married—how would you describe your model of marriage?

A new season, a new model for living needs some new suggestions! Here are some extensive tips and ideas for leadership in the key of life when you are married.

A YEAR OFF FROM WAR?

If a man has recently married, he must not be sent to war or have any other duty laid on him. For one year he is to be free to stay at home and bring happiness to the wife he has married.

DEUTERONOMY 24:5

In some churches I've been part of, some newlywed leaders (both lay leaders and staff) chose to step down from leadership responsibilities for the first year of marriage in order to invest in laying strong foundations in their relationship. The idea was that it was to create space—space to get to know each another and each other's extended families. It was an opportunity to lay down their individual dreams and vision and give time to let a new joint sense of call and purpose emerge. As one friend of mine said, "Your first year of marriage shouldn't have to be about the leadership things you are going to do; it's about getting to know each other, having arguments and having lots of sex!"

When my husband and I got married, we didn't stop working; there was a mortgage and bills to contend with! But we said no to a few more conference invitations and speaking opportunities than usual. Sometimes it was a death to the life I was used to and the leader I was used to being, which was hard at times. Still, it created space for me to understand that I was now part of an "us." My husband was not an add-on to my calling; he *was* my calling. So he was my priority. It sifted out some old ideas, including that I needed to earn God's approval by what I did, and diffused a level of pressure that I was so used to living with that I didn't realize it was there until it wasn't! The season taught me to enjoy his blessings and in time gave birth to a brand new adventure that was far more exciting, challenging and inspiring than anything I could have accomplished alone.

Clearly this will be easier in some professions than others; but what do you think about it as a principle? As busy influential leaders, what could it look like for us to set aside a season where we are more intentional about our marriage and relationships rather than our tasks, roles and dreams?

How would it shape the way we spend our time and emotional energy?

What would it mean for the choices we might make?

For some of us this will come naturally, but for others it comes at huge personal cost. We've invested a lot into our personal careers and we are emotionally involved with them! They've also given back to us in rewarding ways, so we've put them above all else. Marriage has to change that dynamic, because *your husband is your ministry too. He is your calling.*

SET BOUNDARIES, INVEST IN YOUR
RELATIONSHIP AND PROTECT IT

It was interesting to note, when I talked to people, that it was my friends who had been married the longest, often with adult children, who spoke about this the most.

Cathy Moore, now a leadership coach after years leading in the corporate world and in nonprofit organizations, stressed how important it is set boundaries and say no. When Cathy worked as a sales rep for a major IT corporation, she often worked extra-long hours dealing with crises and emergencies in the name of being a team player. "Luckily my husband pulled me up on it and pointed out that I was not coming home for dinner until late and was always breaking home commitments to be at emergency meetings." It was the conversation Cathy needed to take some bold steps. She still worked hard as a team player but set boundaries to prioritize her life at home. She was surprised to see that, although her colleagues were annoyed at first, their respect for her grew because she still worked to a high standard and still delivered results.

Kate Smith also spoke of the need for boundaries:

Sometimes the demarcation of life in ministry and life in the home can be very fuzzy. Inevitably one can end up discussing "work-related" issues over dinner with the family rather than leaving it behind for the day, especially when time is short. This can particularly happen in the bedroom. I recently have told my husband that I don't want to talk about other people and their issues in our most intimate room, especially late at night when it can play on one's mind! Boundaries like this are healthy, especially when there are so many demands on our lives made by other people. Block out time as a couple to "date." Watch a film together, go out for a walk, and if you are in leadership together, try not to talk too much about work!

Suzie Brock, of Wave of Life Ministries, spoke somberly about the need to protect your marriage. "Shared experiences breed intimacy. So you have to be aware of who you are going to share your experiences with." Suzie spoke with a heavy heart about a scenario she'd seen repeatedly over the years. A dynamic leader spends a lot of time on the road. Leading worship here, speaking there, surrounded by a team who become close friends. It's natural, they're together 24/7, working together, serving together, eating and laughing and praying together. But sometimes that leader gets a little too close with another member of the team. Initially it's just a shared joke or a meaningful conversation. But the intimacy is growing while their spouse and children are a world away from this fun, exciting ministry trip. Eventually it goes too far. I've seen it happen so many times," she sighed. Today, when she and her husband, Tom, spend time with leaders, they challenge them to think through how much time they spend away from their family, regardless of how exciting the opportunities are, and to consider bringing their spouses with them sometimes. And if this isn't possible, they encourage leaders to think through ways of still including their spouses in everything that is happening on the road, through phone calls, prayer, conversations. And to be brutally honest with themselves, about their ambition and their ego and their family's needs, to discern how much travel is necessary.

We can also protect our marriages by having regular health checks. Don't let issues drift or grow unchecked. Be proactive over the health of your marriage. Read marriage books together, attend marriage courses that you are *not* leading, take time to ask and process the difficulties in your relationship. I know a couple who, because they were both from very broken homes, were very aware that they approached marriage lacking the example and tools they would have learned in a healthy family environment. Rather than feeling stranded and helpless, or feeling that as leaders they should have it all together, they choose to be proactive and enter seasons of counseling both separately and together, spending time with older married couples to help build the framework of a healthy marriage.

> **Q. How will you set boundaries for your marriage, invest in your marriage, protect your marriage?**

WORKING TOGETHER

What if you and your husband feel called to work together? Marjorie and Nick Allan are leaders at St Thomas Church, Philadelphia, in Sheffield. Having led churches together with her husband for a number of years, here's some advice Marjorie shares:

* Work out "What and who am I called to?" and "What and who is my husband called to?" Sometimes there can be real stress for people in leadership if they are fulfilling a stereotypical role when that isn't necessarily God's call to them, for example a woman trying to operate in church leadership who is called to the workplace or a woman called to church leadership finding herself in the traditional vicar's wife role at home, making cakes. Often we can also put our spouse under pressure by our expectations of him.

* The foundation to living and working together in marriage has to be one of love. Again, you can only arrive at this if you learn to know and operate out of your identity as a much loved child of God. This will enable you to prefer your spouse above yourself, something that is very important if you co-lead. You will learn to be happy when your spouse achieves more for the kingdom than you do. You will also be happy to release him from family life to do what he needs to do.

* After love comes communication, communication, communication. . . . It is an art to be learned and a discipline to maintain.

- Always honor your spouse. This doesn't mean you can't have a difference of opinion—we are happy to publicly disagree in staff meetings, etc., but hopefully from a place of honor. I think this creates an open environment where people are free to ask questions and challenge each other.

- If you lead with your spouse, remain united, but not so united that no one else gets a look in—that's not a fun team to be part of. The kingdom is about community, not a two-man show.

- Compensate for life in the fishbowl: make those necessary deposits in your love tank—love nights away, date nights, chats and a cup of tea, time out, etc.

- Do the regular health checks. What is it like for others to be led by you? What do they actually say? You may think you are "called," but do others? Does your spouse think you are doing well marriage-wise? It might sound obvious, but sadly marriage breakdowns can often come as a surprise to one party. Know who you are or someone else will tell you!

UNITY, NOT COOPERATION

So what if you are both strong characters with strong leadership gifts, significant jobs? Elizabeth is a senior strategic planner for an advertising agency, married to a pioneering church planter and writer, based in West Virginia.

Don't settle for cooperation when God is calling you to unity. That's a lot easier said than done when you have two strong and driven people in a relationship. Doug and I both have apostolic gifts, so there's a lot of vision, dreams and schemes between the two of us. We always supported one another's careers and passion projects, were each the other's biggest fan, helped out when time allowed—but there was very little overlap in what was "ours." After a few years of marriage I realized that we were great at cooperation, but we weren't living one life. That worked when it was just the two of us, but add a baby (or two) to that scenario and the invisible crack becomes a fault line. Once you have kids, there are never enough hours in the day, and since we had more individual vision than family vision, it always felt as though our priorities were competing. We both felt undersupported, overworked, stretched too thin, tired. About a year and a half ago Mike and Sally Breen said something that changed everything for us: *You only get one life, so you should live one life.* They talked about their vision for their family and how everything (jobs, ministry, friends, plans) flowed out of that central vision. What they described wasn't a system of mutual support—it was one of absolute unity. I knew it was the missing piece for us. That was the beginning of us changing a lot about the way we work and operate as a family. It also gave us more opportunities to work on projects together, which we actually found we're really good at. We may debate and disagree during the process (in ways that are pretty comical to watch), but the blending of our gifts can make a pretty powerful combination. Who knew?

FINAL THOUGHTS ON MARRIAGE

Submit to one another out of reverence for Christ.

EPHESIANS 5:21

The one life that Elizabeth speaks of requires mutual submission and sacrifice. Sometimes we'll walk away from wonderful opportunities because it's not the best timing, or because it costs your home life too much. One leader once told me that the leading beat in her family life alternated over the years. There were seasons when her husband's role defined the family's life and rhythm, and she would need to let go of her roles and support him. But then the season would change and she would pick up certain opportunities again. Sacrifice may seem noble from a distance, but it's pretty painful for the one doing the sacrificing! It's important to be honest about that so it doesn't breed resentment in your marriage. We might even feel it's a waste of our God-given gifts and skills. That's when we remind ourselves that marriage is ministry, is our calling too.

MOTHERHOOD AND LEADERSHIP

My husband and I feel as though, whatever else we've been asked or given to do, God entrusted us with the most significant task, the most precious gifts, when he gave us our children. We have two amazing young girls, and I cannot describe the depth of love I have for them. Are motherhood and leadership compatible? When you consider the incredible influence a mother has, it's clear that whatever role she undertakes outside the home, a mother is an incredibly influential woman! It's an awesome calling; mothers shape the world. No one is ever "just a wife and mother," unless you clarify the statement with "just a life-defining, culture-shaping, influential wife and mother"! Today's culture uses language like "working mother" and "stay-at-home/full-time mom," but our lives don't often fit neatly into the boxes such terminology creates. Every mother I've known is a mom full time, and every stay-at-home mom is working very hard full time!

So how do we make life work when motherhood is a part of our leadership and influence? Here are some life lessons from other leaders.

Reflections on Life Lessons

Ali Herbert, leader of Girlzone, St. Mary's Bryanston Square, London:

It's definitely interesting leading anything when you have a young family. In lots of ways it's fantastically life-affirming to be able to spend time leading a group of adults when the rest of your day is spent picking small brightly colored plastic objects off the floor. It's exciting to use your brain again (well, sometimes) and have conversations that

*somehow feel more "important" than, "Hurry up! Clean your teeth!"
But on the other hand, we all know how vital a mother's role in the
family is. Any person can stand up and lead people, but I'm the only
one who can be Mummy to my kids. It won't be like this forever; I can
see them growing up so fast, and I need to remember that now is the
time my input is most important—and also remember to savor and
delight in my role as their mum. The hardest thing I find is the feeling
of rushing from one thing to the next, for instance trying to get the kids
to bed before I rush (unprepared) to a meeting where I'm the one
supposed to be cool, calm and holding things together. I've probably got
spaghetti hoops on my top and it's highly likely I haven't brushed my
hair—so it can be a humbling experience at least! The most important
thing I've found is to try and create a balance. So sometimes it's really
important to say no to things. I'm starting to get better at this now,
even though I sometimes worry I won't be asked again—well, so
what?! Hopefully my identity doesn't rest in whether I'm asked to lead
things or not. And if it does I probably need to do a little heart-
searching. I also need to try and be organized and plan my preparation
in my diary as well as the events themselves. Usually this involves
leaving some leeway with deadlines, in case of situations like a child
being ill, a play date being cancelled or an event at school popping up
in the diary. When my kids were very young I could do little bits and
pieces while they slept—still keeping a bit of time aside for me! Now
that they're at school I have more free (ha!) time and can plan things
more easily. We need to be realistic about how many hours there are in
a day, and know when something life-affirming has become something
life-draining. It's not fair on the children to only leave them the
exhausted parts of us!*

("Only I can be Mom" or "only I can be Grandma" was a line
that came up from a number of these leaders.)

Suzie Brock, of Wave of Life Ministries:

Just because you're called to ministry doesn't mean your kids are! Why should they suffer because you want to travel? We've seen so many children of Christian leaders turned off the church forever because it cost them their parents. We were certain we didn't want to do that, so sought to make choices that would benefit them. We worked out how much travel was healthy for our family, how much time either parent could be away.

Jillian, a social worker before moving into church leadership in a megachurch:

Sometimes the challenge comes when our professional lives are very affirming. People think we're wonderful and tell us we're doing a great job. Meanwhile, our relationships with our children at home may be incredibly difficult, particularly during those teenage years. It's tempting to want to be where the affirmation is, but it's not where you need to be! One of my children was sidelined from the soccer team for a while because of underage drinking. Everyone knew why my daughter was sitting on the bench; and I had to think through whether I cared about what people in the local community thought of me and my parenting. Would I still go to the game, or would I hide at the back so no one saw me? But my daughter needed to know my love and acceptance, regardless of her behavior. So just as I sat nearby and watched her games as things went well, so I sat with her and supported her when she made mistakes.

Does motherhood mean that you can't do as much anymore? Kate Smith says:

There have been times, as the girls have grown up, where as a mum I have stepped away from doing something or going somewhere if I have felt that they needed me or at least one parent around. Sometimes we have to go with the flow and lay some of our own wants and desires aside as individuals, knowing and trusting that our heavenly Father will make up for it in time. It often feels that as a mother we are the one responsible for the children and the home. This has been the case in our marriage, although it is not always the case in every home. I have had to learn to submit to God's process in me and learn that I am not missing out from his hand or his blessing in my life.

Elizabeth, a senior strategic planner in an advertising agency:

The pool of women in the workforce (particularly in senior positions) gets undeniably smaller once children are born. And having started a family myself in the past few years I can't deny that my own priorities have changed in ways that I hadn't fully anticipated. The willingness to put in the kinds of hours that ascent to the most senior positions within a company requires certainly declines—at least for a season. And I believe that many women lack the confidence to return to the workforce after they've stepped out (or eased back) for a while.

My hardest season in leadership was the year after I had our first child. I used to have the time, drive and physical capacity to do whatever it took to get the job done. Routine 65- to 100-hour working weeks, working through the night at the agency, traveling constantly. As long as I was performing at that level, everyone was happy—and while the quality of life wasn't great, the thrill of the challenge and the career advancement helped compensate for the sacrifice.

After our daughter was born, I didn't want to maintain the travel or the hours—and even though I was still doing good work, the "I can do no wrong" mentality I'd experienced before having kids seemed to shift. Like a lot of working mums, I felt for a while that I was failing in all areas of life. Not giving as much as I felt I should at work. Not being as available or present as I felt I should be at home. In reality I wasn't failing at anything, but for someone driven (in all areas of life) and with high (some may say perfectionist) expectations for myself it was a really tough season all round.

SUPERWOMAN, RIP

Would you agree that it's time to retire the notion that we can be good at everything, or that we even need to be good at everything? We set ourselves these unbelievably high standards, often fuelled by guilt, fear, comparison and competition, and wonder why life is so stretching. And they call this "having it all"? I'm not sure those emotions were the "all" that we had in mind! Could it be that we've bought into an ideal that has become an idol that ensnares us? In Scripture we see that when God's people start worshiping idols, it never ends well. Now, we may not be fashioning a golden calf in our dining room. But if we're investing all our emotional energy, prayer and physical efforts into becoming this ideal woman who can do everything, we might need to rethink! Supermom, superwoman, super anything, will let us down some day because it's an unsustainable ideal. So let's not put her up on that pedestal in the first place. As Michele Guinness suggested to me,

> Women can have it all, but not all at once. There's home, work, friends, church and leisure. You can probably manage to juggle around three at any one given time. So don't beat yourself up if one or two have to go on the back burner for a while. They will come round again, even if it's not for a while.

IN PRAISE OF DADS

The way we nurture our children in our culture is a female-determined system—these directions were written by women. It might turn out to be excellent for our children, however, if men have more of an impact on how our kids were raised. We might have healthier children—just as we may have healthier corporations if women were to play a bigger role in them.[1]

Women leaders in church and the workplace acknowledge that to be able to fulfill their call, their husbands must play a larger role in the home and with bringing up the children. It may look different from the world even we grew up in, but it can be a positive thing. When I have traveled in my work, my husband has spent more time on his own with our girls. I may have been traveling to a conference, but for them it's been "Daddy-daughter time." It's required planning and certain sacrifices, but it's been great to see their relationship with him flourish and build lasting memories. Chris does certain things differently from me—for example, the kids are far more adventurous in their play in my absence! But how arrogant is it to assume that my way is the right way or the better way *because I'm a woman?*

Besides, aren't we a team? I wonder if, like me, you forget there are actually two parents, expecting everything to come from me (Superwoman, I said be gone!). There was one day when I struggled with leaving the girls for the day while I went to speak at an event. "I just feel bad about leaving them with someone else," I said. "They're not with someone else," he gently reminded me, "they're with their father. Now go."

We've also grown in appreciation of each other's challenges and gifts as we've shared roles and responsibilities. Ness Wilson, leader of Open Heaven in Loughborough, suggested that we'll need to see flexible models of parenting to create space and time to equip and release gifted women into their calling. "This requires radical servant-secure leadership from men who are married to female leaders."[2]

VILLAGE PEOPLE

The well-worn African proverb "It takes a village to raise a child" is true. As I mentioned earlier, throughout history humanity has formed itself around extended family-sized groups made up of people connected either by blood or purely by relationship. They were both social and economic units. A couple was never intended to raise children alone, but in community. Whatever our sphere of influence, be it in the home, workplace or the church, it's worth thinking and praying through who your village is, or, as we see in the New

Testament, who your *oikos* are. It's fundamental to our effectiveness as influential women. Remember Mrs P. Thirty-One? A closer look at her life reveals that she is a hardworking woman who has a team (Proverbs 31:15). Ali Herbert notes: "It's really key to have a supportive husband or family or friends around—who can help out with practical things like kids' bedtimes or meals, who can pray with you and for you, and who can tell you when you're taking too much on." Marjorie Allan, of St. Thomas', Philadelphia, Sheffield, observed that when you allow others to help you with your home or family matters, this is a blessing for all involved.

> More people mean more support, more wisdom, more skills. Who do you need on your team to make life work? Cleaners, housekeepers, childcare, someone who understands how to run a budget, someone who is good at planning family meals? Some skills you may need to employ, others will be in your community. Pray for them, ask around and seek them out. Accept help and support when it's offered!

It may be vulnerable to invite someone in to help and support us. It challenges our pride to say we need others, but what has it cost when we've lived in isolation as leaders rather than embracing village life?

INFLUENTIAL FAMILIES

Some organizations have a Take Your Child to Work Day, to give children an opportunity to share their parent's world, and perhaps inspire and ignite a few dreams. Perhaps we have the chance as influential women to do the same. Marjorie notes that coleadership has not only given her a very strong foundation in marriage, but has huge potential for blessing as their children grow with kingdom values:

> We believe in including our children on the faith walk, i.e., praying for the sick, giving away money, decisions we make,

etc.—the best inheritance you can ever give them—better than ballet classes!

Noel Brewer Yeatts was taken on her first mission trip by her father when she was just eleven. That and subsequent annual trips marked her life. Today she's the founder of Tour of Hope, a women's movement that inspires and empowers women to make a difference in the developing world.

We can't all have a Take Your Child to Work Day, but we can consider how we influential women have influential marriages and raise influential families.

ONE LIFE

You have one life, and in the end that whole life is ministry. Friendships, marriage, children, work—all of it. How would you like to live it? What would you like to be the legacy of your life choices? It's exciting to be inspired by the ideas and experiences of other women, but you know too that leadership in the key of life, and embracing changing seasons, will mean hard work and sacrifice. It will mean death to ourselves and our ways at times. Are we ready for that? Because it involves the relationships most dear to us, the stakes are high. We don't want to lead at the expense of our marriages and our families, but we're still learning how to develop alternatives.

We're lifelong learners so we will make mistakes. But we'll also make great discoveries. We'll learn. We'll learn to recognize when the seasons change and learn to let go of our visions and dreams in order to embrace reality. We'll learn to pay close attention to the needs of our husbands and families. While we may not have all the details of biblical leaders' lives, the Lord has not left us alone. He's given us a village, and somewhere in that village is a well of wisdom where we can draw near and stay a while. We can sit and talk, ask questions, seek advice, share our stories and be refreshed for the days ahead. Have you drawn from the well of wisdom in your community yet?

Reflections on Leadership

Rebecca Lindsay, church planter, Switzerland:

A challenge is always not separating my different roles—like, now I'm a mother, now I'm a wife . . . now a leader. I think being a woman in leadership is involving the different parts together, so that the different parts can have a positive impact on each other.

Samantha, married to a pastor, two children:

Keeping the lines of communication open is essential—when you have small children, a job and a ministry all vying for your time, it's easy to sweep a few things under the carpet, but with so much pressure in life, it doesn't take much for the lumps under the carpet to cause you to stumble!

And a word for the clergy wives from Hannah Absalom, married to Alex, a pastor in Ohio, mother to three boys:

Many expectations will be placed on you. Don't do stuff because it's expected; don't fall into the trap of doing what other people want, but only do what Jesus says!

Don't let others get to your spouse through you. Obviously, there will be times when you can help people, but particularly when people have an "issue" with something/your spouse, don't let them go through you!

Don't take it personally when people let you down!

Being positive, you will have amazing opportunities, friends and relationships!

The Art of Living Skillfully

Leadership will never just be fully handed to you in a
neat little package. Every woman you see leading has done a lot of
hard work in their hearts and in their community to be there.

JORDANNE BONFIELD, EQUIPPING PASTOR,
THE GATHERING NETWORK, KANSAS CITY

Wisdom is the art of living skillfully in
whatever actual conditions we find ourselves.

EUGENE PETERSON, INTRODUCTION TO THE
BOOK OF PROVERBS IN *THE MESSAGE*

WE'RE NEARLY AT THE END OF OUR JOURNEY. Look how far
we've come.

We saw that, all around the world, women of all colors, classes and
creeds are influencing, leading and shaping their communities. But
women in the Western church have received conflicting messages on
where influence fits for them. So we went back to our roots and reac-
quainted ourselves with Eve, the blueprint for women. We then looked
at our God-given design and identity, the *ezer*, discovering there is more
to us than we dreamed, or maybe hoped for, and that God delights in it
all. We've identified a number of different ways to seek God about his
call on our lives. Then we turned our attention to some interior work,

as we learned that our character is more important than our gifts and abilities. We need to be whole and attend to the broken pieces of our lives so that our capacity to lead isn't undermined by our brokenness.

We've seen again that leadership is not for lone rangers; we don't have to do this alone. We can be supported, encouraged and accountable. But for this to happen we need to develop healthy relationships with female peers, and to get creative about searching for mentoring. When it comes to working alongside men, it's helpful to know the filter through which we view them, and to be aware of how to navigate a predominantly male working world. Leadership isn't a lineal experience, especially for women. The different seasons and stages of life present us with new challenges and opportunities to serve him. We need to engage and embrace the death and the life found in each season, if we hope to continue to grow and mature.

Yet we've only scratched the surface of the subject of leadership! There is so much deeper, further that we could go, so many tools and skills out there that we can discover. One essential skill that we'll all need, regardless of our sphere of influence, is wisdom. Perhaps it's odd to think of wisdom as a skill; wise people just seem to *know* so much. However, wisdom is not information or knowledge, but is found in the ability to apply the things we've learned in our everyday lives. As personified in the book of Proverbs, wisdom is bold, calling out in the public arena for the opportunity to practically guide people's lives (Proverbs 1:20). Wisdom is described as one who protects people from temptations that ensnare them (Proverbs 2:12), and offers a prosperity that moves beyond even jewels and riches. Actively involved in the earth's creation (Proverbs 3:19), wisdom continues to affirm and enrich life. And as if the Father wanted to offer a sweet affirmation of his *ezer*s, when he personifies wisdom in his Word he makes wisdom a *she*. Oh, how he loves us.[1]

So wisdom (or *sophia* as she is known in the Greek) is earthy and practical. As Eugene Peterson so eloquently puts it, wisdom is "the art of living skillfully in whatever actual conditions we find ourselves."

With this in mind, this closing chapter offers a few final tips and insights that leaders have gleaned while learning *the art of skillful living*. Remember that skillful living is an art that is learned in the life of every leader, male or female. None of us has it all together. You'll see that a number of these insights have been learned the hard way. Some skills were fashioned in difficult places; the leader didn't realize that wisdom was forming at the time. Years later they offer the life-affirming, life-enriching wisdom that benefits others. I hope you find them helpful.

KEEP YOURSELF WELL

Be yourself, but make sure you understand yourself and are self-aware. Take every personality profile test, get analyzed, whatever helps you discover how you're wired. Know what makes you tick, how you communicate, what upsets you. Don't allow the workplace to be all-consuming. Live a balanced life and take care of yourself—physically, emotionally and spiritually. (Beth Fitch, an Arizona-based business entrepreneur, a founding partner of Righi Hernandez law firm and a leader in Alpha USA. She is married with two sons.)

Leaders are notorious for taking care of everyone else. We can be aware of and in tune with the needs, strengths and weaknesses of those around us, yet be oblivious to our own. We've already acknowledged how the past and our wounds can affect our potential for influence. In addition, it's good to be in tune with our emotions, aware of what brings us joy or pain. We also need to attend to how we are physically, from the impact of our menstrual cycle to our personal fitness levels. It's important to pay attention to our whole life.

Here's Marie's story:

I continually have to work at remaining healthy. I've found that in Christian leadership I have often become too busy, and have not taken time to rest and look after myself. I have at times neglected sleep, not blocked out time to exercise and have often used comfort eating as a way to deal with stress. None of these actions are good and in the long term can limit your leadership capacity. Leadership is demanding, there is no getting away from it, but if you want to stay in it for the long haul, it's vital that we take time to look after our bodies by watching our diets, exercising regularly and making sure we get enough sleep. To be healthy we also need to pay attention to our emotional needs—it's important that we make time for work and play. It's all too easy to end up with an unbalanced life, trying to juggle various balls, whether that is running a home, looking after children, doing a second job. It can be challenging to fit everything in, but my advice would be to make sure you do some things for you. We need to remember that God isn't just interested in what you do for him—he's actually interested in every aspect of who we are.

Do you look after yourself? One simple way you can look after yourself is to uphold the fourth commandment and take a day off every week. "You can't cheat the Sabbath," Vineyard leader Steve Nicholson said to our leadership team in Sheffield many years ago. "Before you know it, you'll be running on adrenalin. You won't even know how tired you are. But you'll start making decisions as though you were drunk. Take your day off and keep taking your day off." This was one of those nuggets of wisdom that stayed with me, and is a line that I keep on returning to, either for myself or for others. A day off seems like such a small thing. But we need regular renewal and refreshment—remember HALT?

Are you bad at taking your day off? Are you so busy looking after the needs of your husband and kids that there is no time to rest? If so, invite someone to hold you accountable to carve out space for the rest and time out you need. Make sure also that you rest in ways that refresh and vitalize you. Along the same lines, make sure you take all your holiday allocation in the year. One way to ensure this actually happens is to block out your holiday dates at the start of a year so that it's in the system at work.

Alongside a regular day off, it's important that we learn how to switch off. Mobile phones and social media give us great opportunities to connect with people all the time. I love it that I can Skype my brother in Hong Kong, and then Facebook chat with friends in the U.K. moments later. But sometimes the best way we can take care of ourselves and get some space is to switch off and step back from it all. Yes, that email can wait, as can that phone call. So can that tweet or that YouTube clip. The wonders of modern technology can be energizing, but too much of a good thing can distract you from your priorities or drain your energy supply. To give your best to your sphere of influence, you'll need to be focused and vital and engaged. You need to be healthy.

Susan Martins Miller, author, lay leader, wife and mother, agrees:

> The best thing you can do for anyone—whether your family or your ministry—is to be aware of your own wellness. By this I mean seeing yourself as a whole person, body and spirit, in relationship to God. This doesn't mean everything is hunky-dory in your life. It won't be. But what things are you doing for yourself to be nourished and refreshed in both body and spirit in spite of the things that don't go according to plan? The balance between family and leadership is not always perfect equilibrium. One arena or another may be more demanding for a season. But you are no good to anyone if you are a run-down, malnourished, sleepless, relationshipless wreck. Keep yourself well.

BODY TALK

People will take you as seriously as you take yourself. Project an image of confidence and authority. (Elizabeth Paul, senior strategic planner for an advertising agency)

Remember that your body talks. In fact, it speaks a lot more than your words do. Is it communicating what you're actually trying to say? Think about your posture, your facial expressions and your tone of voice. Do they communicate confidence—or inadequacy? Can you stand tall with your head lifted up? Do you struggle to look directly at people? Think about how you can improve your body talk. A smile goes a long way!

Does it matter how you look? Or should you be free to dress however you want?

Cathy discovered that it did matter! She was a tall, blond, fresh-faced sales executive for a major printing company, and turned up at an old steel mill in Texas immaculately dressed in her business suit and heels. No one took her seriously; they humored her and ignored what she had to say.

As I drove away I remembered the old marketing professor's college advice of "dress like your customer, so always have a change of clothes with you." So in a time when corporate women did not wear trousers, in the middle of nowhere I squiggled out of my skirt and into my matching suit trousers and went back into that steel mill, donned my hard hat, and was given the real tour and taken more seriously. They listened because I looked as if I belonged. My company was not impressed, until I brought in the business!

Cathy concluded,

Pay attention to what you wear—it does matter. Do not wear clothes that show too much sexuality or you will be seen as a plaything. Men will make you feel a team player, but you are a sex object, not a teammate. Women will not respect you.

Michele Guinness says:

Help yourself feel confident by knowing you look your best. If you don't know what your best is, get one or two friends whose taste you trust to help you choose an outfit or two. Do dress appropriately. Men and women always appreciate it when someone has made an effort for them. And first appearances are important. Ensure you feel comfortable in what you're wearing, but remember, small heels, earrings and a spot of make-up will mean you're taken more seriously. Remember, younger women are looking for role models. They don't want to think that being a Christian means dowdy and boring.

Anne Maclaurin suggests:

If you struggle with body image or self-image problems then get them sorted out. Get prayer and counsel about it. Also be practical and go shopping with friends. If you're uncertain of what to do, consider having your color chart done to discover what looks good on you.

Anne sums it up when she says, "Dress well, eat well, live right."

USE YOUR HEAD!

Wise leaders take time to evaluate the condition of their mind. Is it being sharpened to a razor's edge or becoming a bowl of mush?[2]

Find good resources that speak to your sphere of influence. Look at blogs and websites, listen to podcasts, and read books and leadership magazines. Learn from different generations of leaders, or leaders from different cultures. Allow your mind to be stretched with a perspective beyond what you already know. I like to go to the business section in bookshops because I often find great resources on women in leadership there. The business world has made strides in understanding the nuances concerning women in leadership in some areas that the church hasn't, and there are women who are veterans in business with vast experience. I also read lots of Christian leadership books. They may not specifically address women, nor do they exclude us. So dig in. Ask the leaders around you what they're reading, what they're listening to. That will also give you insights into the culture of where you work.

Whether you work for a church or in the business world, work out your theology of leadership and of women in leadership. You know, there are lots of views out there, all held by wonderful people. Do the groundwork on establishing your understanding of Scripture. At some point it will be tested, and you will need to know what you're standing on because, so often in those moments, you'll stand alone. It's hard work, but it's a vital investment of your time and energy in God's purpose for your life. You don't want to your limit your capacity for leadership and influence just because you never took the time to invest your intellect into your theological views. Leadership is challenging enough as it is, without a grinding insecurity about God's perspective on your life. So give your brain a workout! If you don't know where to look, there are some resources at the end of the book. Some will be websites which are free, others books which are a small price to pay for what you'll receive. You'll also need to learn how to respectfully disagree with those who disagree with you.

DEVELOP YOUR SKILLS

Cherish the gifts you have been given—seek to grow in them and develop them constantly through learning, experience, and prayer asking the Holy Spirit all along the way to keep teaching you how and what God has made you. (Tom and Sue Brawner. Tom is the associate pastor of Heartland Community Church, Kansas.)

Thomas Edison, the American inventor, said that genius is one percent inspiration and ninety-nine percent perspiration. He understood that even our gifts and raw talent need honing and sharpening. We need to keep investing in our gifts and abilities. We can develop our skills in a wide range of ways.

Consider what training courses, classes or resources are available that will invest in your leadership skills. For example, Michele Guinness suggests, "If you're going to do public speaking, don't sniff at some voice/drama training. It will help with voice projection, timings and how to use eye contact."

Beth Fitch advises that leaders should get in the habit of evaluating and reevaluating how effective they are in their role, remaining open to change where needed. However, in order to evaluate effectively we need to be sufficiently humble and secure to invite others into the evaluation process. Learn to value feedback from people around you. Michele Guinness suggests:

> Get feedback from someone you trust implicitly, not from someone who might be tempted to be a little jealous of you (and believe me, women are when they see one of the sisterhood step into the limelight—it's our besetting sin!). Use all criticism as constructive. Let it help you to grow, rather than crush your spirit. If you are never criticized, you probably aren't changing anything.

Much as we hope and expect that our leadership development will come through positions and personal opportunities, we often develop our skills serving someone else's position and opportunities for a season. As a speaker and communicator, one of the best training experiences for me was doing some research for my vicar's sermons. I had access to his library of books. I had lots of opportunity to listen to his thoughts and ideas on what he was preaching. Over the space of two years, I learned huge amounts about how to communicate and to seek God on how to preach his Word without saying a word to anyone publicly. Just because our role may be public doesn't mean all of our mentoring and training needs to be.

People skills are often underestimated, but are essential for leadership. We've already explored some of our working relationships, and we've seen that Matthew 18 offers us guidelines for healthy conflict resolution. One key area we can reflect on as we seek to develop our people skills is the area of communication. Aware of how hard good communication can be, particularly when broaching difficult subjects, Elizabeth offers a simple practical approach for our conversations: "Be sensitive in how you dish it. Be objective in how you take it." Yet in our technological world, communication is not only verbal but expressed in voicemails, texts, tweets, emails, Facebook status . . . And we communicate with our silence too! We've got so many opportunities to communicate well and communicate badly! Are you a great communicator over coffee but never get around to sending a follow-up email because you prefer to work face to face? Are you efficient with social media but not so skilled in tangible relationships? Prayerfully consider how your communication strengths and weaknesses impact your effectiveness as a leader. What skills do you need to develop? Beth advises that leaders need to study human behavior and different communication styles in order to sharpen our people skills.

ANOTHER VITAL SKILL:
LEARN HOW TO SAY NO

Resist the temptation to let others pigeonhole you into areas that are not of your gifting—rather, be appropriately assertive (confidence with humility) about making your gifts, passions and serving desires known. (Tom and Sue Brawner)

Every job has the tasks that no one likes. These tasks are not our passion, but they're a necessary part of being a leader and we just get on with them. However, sometimes we find ourselves perpetually undertaking tasks that are not normally our responsibility or that do not reflect our gifts and call. We give more to a project than required, give more hours than we should to get something done, and it's not about being a team player: it's a reflection of our chronic inability to say no. "No" is an incredibly easy word to say, in theory.

Yet whether you're a parent or a chief executive or both, it seems to be a word that disappears from our vocabulary, especially when we are trying to keep someone happy or want them to go away! We neglect the boundaries that we spoke of in earlier chapters and overload ourselves. Sometimes our desire to be wanted, liked and approved gets us worn out. Learn how to say no. Perhaps start by making a general principle of not saying yes to anything immediately, giving yourself a day to reply. I found the space helped me formulate the words more easily. Sometimes people would request an immediate answer, which would be responded to with an immediate need to go to the restroom. Anything to buy more time! I worked on a sentence that I could say easily, which was positive, polite, but definitely a no. Over time, as I worked on people-pleasing tendencies, it was much easier. I just needed somewhere to begin.

Where do you need to begin?

LEARN FROM THE GREATEST LEADER THAT EVER WALKED THE EARTH

Keep your eyes on Jesus, who both began and finished this race we're in. Study how he did it.

(HEBREWS 12:2 THE MESSAGE)

We're used to Jesus the friend, Jesus the Savior, Jesus the Lord. Do you know Jesus the leader yet? Jesus was the greatest leader that ever walked the earth. Have you studied his life to see his art of skillfull living, to explore what leadership can truly be?

There are so many things we can learn from Jesus the leader. We noted earlier in the book that we see three main priorities expressed in Jesus' life: a relationship with the Father, authentic relationships with other believers, and a relationship to the world around himself expressed in an active missionary life of evangelism and service. These priorities defined the type of leader Jesus was and is.

First, we see that, for Jesus, leadership meant radical dependence on the Father. He was a leader whose decisions were led by the One who led him. He led—yes, was constantly led—by this key relationship. Jesus was incredibly powerful, but he didn't rely on his charisma or powers of persuasion. His words, works and deeds as a leader were empowered by the presence of the Holy Spirit. I find it so easy to get ahead of myself with my ideas of what could and should be. After all, I'm the leader, I'm supposed to know the answers, know what to do, right? Not quite. Jesus the leader demonstrates what it looks like to depend on the Father entirely as we lead, doing what we see God doing, being where he is (John 5:19). Wise leadership makes space for the Father's voice, and welcomes the Spirit's power.

Second, we see that Jesus the leader not only makes room for authentic relationships, but that his leadership empowers others to realize their potential. Though Jesus was sinless and the most skilled, most effective leader, he was completely committed to working with a team. He spent all night praying about who he should gather into his core team (Luke 6). Jesus did life with his team, and he generally sent his disciples out in teams of two, whether it was for a mission trip (Matthew 10) or to get a donkey (Luke 19). It is clear to see that Jesus didn't have his disciples sitting around doing nothing, watching the expert at work. Jesus entrusted them with responsibilities; they learned on the job with him. When I apply this to my own areas of responsibility I'm challenged to pray for the people I work with and about whom to mentor. It reminds me that leadership is not just about my opportunities, my role and my chance to shape something. Some of us have been waiting for our calling and our gifts to be validated for so long that we find it hard to empower others, feeling that we've barely had our own turn! Jesus demonstrates that leadership continually raises up new leaders in tangible ways, and we rejoice if they go further than we ever could. We'll need to be secure to follow his example, but Christian leaders in the workplace and the church recognize that raising up new leaders is integral to their understanding of leadership:

Servant leadership is key. It's important that leaders are constantly looking to implement methods to empower those around them to thrive and succeed. (Beth Fitch)

You can't do it all yourself: give it away. Leadership is about inspiring, influencing and releasing other people—those who are following—to help them be the best they can be, creating space for them to succeed. That's servant leadership. (Gareth Robinson)

Third, Jesus was focused on the job God had called him to do. The first chapter of Mark's Gospel recounts the incredible events surrounding the start of Jesus' ministry in Capernaum. The tone is fast-paced and dynamic. Jesus teaches with an authority that no one has seen before. He drives out a demon and heals Simon's mother-in-law. The events of the day electrify the community, so much so that by the evening the entire town has gathered outside the door of Simon's home, where Jesus is based, and Jesus heals the sick and drives out demons. What an incredible breakthrough! Early the next morning Jesus retreats to pray. When the disciples finally locate him, ready for another day of action-packed ministry and miracles in Capernaum, Jesus says:

"Let us go somewhere else—to the nearby villages—so I can preach there also. That is why I have come." So he traveled throughout Galilee, preaching in their synagogues and driving out demons. (Mark 1:38-39)

What would you have wanted to do in Jesus' position? I know I would have wanted to stay in Capernaum for a while—after all, the work had been so successful. It seems Jesus had a different definition of success. His understanding of success was found in his obedience to what God wanted him to do, not what the results of his obedience were. Throughout the Gospels we see that Jesus was entirely focused on his mission to seek and save the lost and head toward Jerusalem to bring salvation to all humanity. Temptation would not cause him to stumble. His critics and detractors could never engage him for long; Jesus kept his focus throughout.

What is your focus? Are you doing what God has called you to do? Are you taking your place in his story or are you diverted by what others are doing? Consider what distracts you; observe what dissipates your resolve. Have we become preoccupied with opinions and debate, who we please or offend? For Christian leaders it's easy to become more preoccupied with the church's culture and its quirks rather than heeding its commission to make disciples in a broken world. Alternatively we may have grown comfortable in the success we've already experienced, and lost motivation. Don't lose sight of what God has called you to do—do it.

Let the greatest leader who ever walked the earth lead you onward. Humbly pay attention to his life, because that is where wisdom begins:

> Skilled living gets its start in the Fear-of-GOD,
>   insight into life from knowing a Holy God. (Proverbs 9:10
> *The Message*)

Follow his example. Follow him.

Follow Him

As Jesus and his disciples were on their way, he came to a village where
a woman named Martha opened her home to him. She had a sister called
Mary, who sat at the Lord's feet listening to what he said. But Martha was
distracted by all the preparations that had to be made. She came to him
and asked, "Lord, don't you care that my sister has left me to
do the work by myself? Tell her to help me!"

LUKE 10:38-42

CAN'T THEY SEE THAT I NEED SOME HELP OVER HERE?
I can imagine Martha's frustration. There were jobs to be done.
There were *always* jobs to be done, and a guest like him was no ordinary
guest. There were things to do, preparations to be made when Jesus was
around. To make him welcome, make him feel at home. Somewhere to
rest and relax after all his travels, somewhere to meet and talk with the
Twelve if needed. Something always happened when Jesus was around.
You had to be prepared. There was so much to be done, and Mary was
doing none of it. No, instead of her customary role of helping, she is
sitting at Jesus' feet, listening to every word he says. Martha understands
that Jesus is great to listen to, but has nobody else noticed that she's been
left to organize *everything*? Perhaps Martha wouldn't have to be such a,
well, *Martha* if a certain sister named Mary was pulling her weight!

There are so many things we can learn from these wonderful
sisters in the Gospels. They're committed and they're faithful to

Jesus. Martha's story does remind us that at times we're simply too busy to connect with Jesus, learn from Jesus, simply be with Jesus. Her lesson in this moment reminds us that while there are lots of incredibly important things to be done *for* Jesus, we also need to be *with* Jesus, invest in our relationship with him. Martha's life speaks to influential women and men everywhere. Sometimes the stuff of life can consume us all and we are much poorer for it. We need to stay connected to our Source of life and our Reason for living.

Remember in the end who this is all about. Invest in your relationship with him. Nurture and protect it, work at it. Spend time with him. Worship him, pray to him, live your life in the light of him. Dive into the depths of his Word, and hear the love letter of the Father to his children. Consider Jesus, look at his life, remember what he won for you on the cross. Remember that the Holy Spirit is not the optional extra in the Trinity. Invite him to be the Paraclete that Scripture says he is, one who comes alongside you in everyday life, and keep on being filled with his life and power (Ephesians 5:18).

I look at Mary and I'm inspired. She wanted to be with Jesus, listen to Jesus, learn from Jesus. Her example gives me pause at the start of the day and throughout the busyness of the day, to remember him and to be with him, to listen to him. Her example has saved me from ill-advised words and ill-timed actions. A moment with him and he's touched my heart again and reset my course.

Yet what I've never seen in Mary's actions until now is her courage. Mary knew her place in her culture in her home. Michele Guinness notes that "though Jewish women were educated, it was their duty to run the home. Theological study, to sit at the rabbi's feet and learn, was a male prerogative."[1] And yet there Mary was. Of course she was aware that she had left Martha to do all the work; Martha would not have needed to heave deep sighs and bang around in the kitchen to get the message across. I wonder if Mary wrestled with fleeting moments of guilt that day. Had she abandoned her responsibilities as a woman? Of course she was aware that she was adopting a position, the position of a disciple, more commonly reserved for men in her community. And it was quite a position that she had chosen to adopt. A rabbi's disciples were more than academic students. They followed the rabbi closely so they'd know how to live. They sought to imitate every aspect of their rabbi's life. In time the process of imitation led to the disciple himself becoming a rabbi, with followers who would complete the same journey. So who did Mary think she was, anyway? Was she trying to be one of the boys? Did she intend to be like Jesus, to preach and pray, to heal the sick and cast out demons? To do what all the other disciples did? Was she ambitious? We simply don't know. But I wonder if she felt embarrassed, self-conscious, even rebellious and disrespectful for the choice she made. In the end it seemed that it wasn't who Mary thought she was or hoped to be that determined her choice that day: it was about who she knew Jesus was. Her actions were a response to him, and as his follower first and foremost, she needed to be where he was. So in the face of convention she sat in the posture of a disciple and she followed him.

Now it's our turn. Like Mary we need to sit at Jesus' feet and listen. We need to hear his voice speaking to us clearly, because like Mary we'll need courage.

We need courage to be the women Jesus calls and commissions us to be, so that we too can break with convention when necessary to step into his plan for our lives. We need to be brave enough to walk away from expectations and limitations that hold us back, even our own. We need to be secure enough to live as the *ezers* he intended.

We'll need courage to face the challenges of our day, to walk into dark places and be the light, to go to countless lives that are rotting away and be the salt. We'll need patience and compassion to rebuild a broken society. We'll also need to be bold and imaginative to take hold of the opportunities that are right in front of us. People are hungry for spiritual things, for genuine community, for causes worth living for. We are influential. We're women in leadership in the church, in our homes, at work and beyond. So, sisters, it's time to rise up. Take your visions and dreams, your strategic minds and your skills, your hospitality and your hearts, your lives and your love and go . . .

Go and make his love visible.

Notes

Introduction

[1]"Top Ten Most Influential Britons in America," *Daily Telegraph*, January 10, 2008.

[2]Belinda Luscombe, "The Rise of the Sheconomy," *Time*, November 22, 2010, p. 58.

[3]Eleanor Frances Hall, *Florence Nightingale* (New York: Macmillan, 1920), p. 74.

[4]Edwin Friedman, *A Failure of Nerve: Leadership in the Age of the Quick Fix*, ed. Margaret M. Treadwell and Edward W. Beal (New York: Seabury, 2007).

[5]Loren Cunningham and David Joel Hamilton, *Why Not Women?* (Seattle: YWAM Publishing, 2000), p. 68.

[6]Interview with Danielle Stickland, *Christianity*, March 2010, p. 20.

Chapter 1: The Blueprint

[1]Carolyn Custis James, *Lost Women of the Bible: The Women We Thought We Knew* (Grand Rapids: Zondervan, 2005), p. 29.

[2]R. David Freeman, "Woman: A Power Equal to Man," *Biblical Archaeology Review* 9 (1983): 56-58.

[3]Walter Kaiser, "Correcting Caricatures: The Biblical Teaching on Women," *Priscilla Papers* 19, no. 2 (Spring 2005): 5-11.

[4]Michele Guinness, *Woman: The Full Story* (Grand Rapids: Zondervan, 2003), p. 34.

[5]Kaiser, "Correcting Caricatures," pp. 5-6.

[6]Freeman, "Woman: A Power Equal to Man," pp. 56-58.

[7]James, *Lost Women of the Bible*, p. 37.

Chapter 2: The Cloud of Witnesses

[1]Linda L. Belleville, "Women Leaders in the Bible," in *Discovering Biblical Equality*, ed. Ronald W. Pierce, Rebecca Merrill Groothuis and Gordon Fee (Downers Grove, Ill.: InterVarsity Press, 2005), p. 111.

[2]Ibid., p. 113.

[3]Dorothy L. Sayers, *Are Women Human?* (Downers Grove, Ill.: InterVarsity Press, 1975), p. 47.

[4]D. M. Scholer, "Women," in *Dictionary of Jesus and the Gospels,* ed. Joel B. Green, Scot McKnight and I. Howard Marshall (Downers Grove, Ill.: Inter-Varsity Press, 1992), p. 882.

[5]Craig Evans, *Luke,* New International Biblical Commentary (Peabody, Mass.: Hendrickson, 1990), p. 122.

[6]Carolyn Custis James, *Lost Women of the Bible* (Zondervan, 2005), p. 199.

[7]Scholer, "Women," p. 886.

[8]Mike Breen and Steve Cockram, *Building a Discipling Culture* (n.p.: 3DM Publishing, 2009), p. 107.

[9]Romans 16:3-5.

[10]Taken from Loren Cunningham and David Joel Hamilton, *Why Not Women?* (Seattle: YWAM Publishing, 2000), p. 145. Originally John Chrysostom, "First Homily on the Greeting to Priscilla and Aquila," trans. Catherine Clark Kroeger, *Priscilla Papers* 5, no. 3 (Summer 1991): 18.

[11]Quoted in Belleville, "Women Leaders in the Bible," p. 118.

[12]Ibid., p. 117.

[13]Rodney Stark, *The Rise of Christianity: How the Obscure, Marginal Jesus Movement Became the Dominant Religious Force in the Western World in a Few Centuries* (New York: HarperOne, 1997), p. 108.

[14]Michele Guinness, *Woman: The Full Story* (Grand Rapids: Zondervan, 2003), p. 121.

[15]Cunningham and Hamilton, *Why Not Women?* p. 151.

[16]Belleville, "Women Leaders in the Bible," p. 123.

[17]Guinness, *Woman: The Full Story,* p. 120.

[18]*Analytical Greek Lexicon* (Bagster, 1870), p. 385.

[19]Ben and Ann Witherington, *Women and the Genesis of Christianity* (Cambridge: Cambridge University Press, 1990), p. 186.

[20]Richard Kroeger and Catherine Kroeger, *I Suffer Not a Woman: Rethinking 1 Timothy 2:11-15 in Light of Ancient Evidence* (Grand Rapids: Baker Books, 1992), p. 75.

[21]Ibid., p. 98.

[22]Scot McKnight, "Women Ministering" <www.cbeinternational.org/files/u1/women-ministering.pdf>.

Chapter 3: Calling

[1]This observation stems from Mike Breen and Steve Cockram, *Building a Discipling Culture* (n.p.: 3DM Publishing, 2009), and is further expounded in that

book and in my *Real God, Real Life* (London: Hodder & Stoughton, 2010).

[2]Stephen R. Covey, *The Seven Habits of Highly Effective People* (New York: Simon & Schuster, 1989), p. 98.

[3]Mike Breen, *Continuous Breakthrough* (n.p.: 3DM Publishing, 2009), p. 100.

[4]Ibid., p. 103.

[5]If you want to look at this more closely and get into the theology behind it more than we've got time for here, check out the following resources: Mike Breen and Steve Cockram, *Building a Discipling Culture*; Mike Breen, *The Apostle's Notebook* (Kingsway, 2002; one of a series of books on each aspect of the fivefold ministry); and see <www.weare3DM.com> for questionnaires and PDFs that help you look at the roles in more detail.

Chapter 4: A Tale of Two Queens

[1]Read about Jezebel and her dealings with Ahab and Elijah in 1 Kings 18–19; 21–22.

[2]Carolyn Custis James, *Lost Women of the Bible* (Grand Rapids: Zondervan, 2005), p. 148.

Chapter 5: Coming to a Halt

[1]"Zimri" is a reference to a military leader in 1 Kings 16 who seized the throne and was killed seven days later.

[2]Ronald Heifetz and Marty Linsky, *Leadership on the Line: Staying Alive Through the Dangers of Leading* (Boston: Harvard Business School Press, 2002), p. 180.

[3]Ibid., p. 164.

Chapter 6: Broken in God's House

[1]This understanding of "covenant" has come from Mike Breen, *Covenant and Kingdom: The DNA of the Bible* (n.p.: 3DM Publishing, 2010), pp. 21-36.

[2]In the Greek text, a more accurate reading is "to be filled and go on being filled with the Holy Spirit."

Chapter 7: Influential Relationships

[1]The idea of a labyrinth of choices comes from Alice H. Eagly and Linda L. Carli, *Through the Labyrinth: The Truth About How Women Become Leaders* (Boston: Harvard Business School Press, 2007).

[2]Taken from Danielle Strickland, "Developing Women," *Youthwork*, 2007, p. 21.

[3]The huddle questions are available as free downloads from <www.weare3dm .com> in the resources section—*go and get them!* There are other huddle resources too.

Chapter 8: Navigating a Man's World

[1] Gail Evans, *Play Like a Man, Win Like a Woman* (New York: Broadway Books, 2000), pp. 19-22.

[2] Lois P. Frankel, *Nice Girls Don't Get the Corner Office: 101 Unconscious Mistakes Women Make That Sabotage Their Careers* (New York: Hachette Book Group, 2010), p. xvi.

[3] Evans, *Play Like a Man, Win Like a Woman*, p. 11.

[4] Alice H. Eagly and Linda L. Carli, *Through the Labyrinth: The Truth About How Women Become Leaders* (Boston: Harvard Business School Press, 2007), p. 137.

[5] Ibid.

[6] Lois Frankel suggests a similar set of ideas in *Nice Girls Don't Get the Corner Office*, p. 21.

[7] Eagly and Carli, *Through the Labyrinth*, p. 144.

Chapter 9: Leadership in the Key of Life

[1] Linda L. Belleville, "Women Leaders in the Bible," in *Discovering Biblical Equality*, ed. Ronald W. Pierce, Rebecca Merrill Groothuis and Gordon Fee (Downers Grove, Ill.: InterVarsity Press, 2005), p. 122.

[2] Taken from "Do You Fancy a Coffee Sometime?" which I wrote with my friend Sally Breen, in *Worth Knowing: Wisdom for Women*, ed. Ali Herbert (London: Survivor, 2007), p. 52.

Chapter 10: A Change in Season

[1] Gail Evans, *Play Like a Man, Win Like a Woman* (New York: Broadway Books, 2000), p. 12.

[2] Michele Guinness, "The Stained Glass Ceiling," *Christianity*, March 2010, p. 27.

Chapter 11: The Art of Living Skillfully

[1] This feminine personification of wisdom is also seen in Jesus' reference to wisdom in Matthew 11:19.

[2] Kevin Harney, *Leadership from the Inside Out* (Grand Rapids: Zondervan, 2007), p. 57.

Chapter 12: Follow Him

[1] Michele Guinness, *Woman: The Full Story* (Grand Rapids: Zondervan, 2003), p. 116.

Group Discussion Guide

More Than Enchanting is intended to help women understand and use their influence better. The following questions have been prepared to help your group break through barriers to influence your world.

1. Jo writes that Jesus' "understanding of success was found in his obedience to what God wanted him to do, not what the results of his obedience were" (p. 193). How important are results in situations where you exercise influence? What is your definition of a successful leader?

2. Jo writes on page 38, "*Ezers* are fighters—for their friends, their families, their communities, their churches, their nations. But their strength doesn't cost them their womanhood, their femininity. They've learned that their strength is feminine. You see, it's part of their God-given design." Where have you seen women fight for those around them? What made their strength distinctly feminine?

3. Jo writes, "What would it look like if we . . . embraced the call to a God-infused life? If we explored the implications of the call or vocation of being a friend, wife, mother, child? Or being a member of that team at work? Would we live differently? Pray differently, act differently? Would it redefine our use of time, money and effort? When relationships were strained, would we be more likely to see whether reconciliation was possible? What if we attended to our jobs as though they were our God-given vocation? Or engaged with our churches as if they were the

204 MORE THAN ENCHANTING

community the Lord himself had given us?" How does thinking
of your responsibilities in the context of a "call or vocation" affect the way you approach them?

4. Jo suggests that the quality of Jezebel's and Esther's leadership
came not from personal skills or charisma but from "what is happening in their hearts" (p. 82). Where do you think Jezebel went
wrong? Where did Esther go right? How can we be more like
Esther today?

5. What gets in the way of finding our security "in God rather
than what people say or think about us" (p. 86)? What helps you
look to God rather than others for validation?

6. "HALT—Hungry, Angry, Lonely, Tired—is an acronym used in
recovery groups and stress management classes as a self-assessment
tool to equip people to be aware of their basic needs and vulnerabilities" (p. 88). Reflect for a moment on which part of the
HALT acronym is most relevant to your life right now. How can
you practically work toward fullness and healing in these areas?

7. What are some of the challenges for single women in ministry?
What about married women?

8. Is loneliness the cost for Christian women to break through into
positions of leadership (see p. 9 8)? What are some practical ways
for all people to move out of loneliness and into noncompetitive,
life-giving relationships?

9. What does it mean to you that we can come to God's house "as
we are, not as we feel we ought to be" (p. 106)? Do you think
many Christians embrace this? Why or why not? What would it
mean for your life and ministry if you did?

10. Could you relate to any of the women "navigating a man's
world" (see pp. 141-42)? What are some of the challenges you've
faced in these areas? How have you dealt with such challenges?
What's helped you deal with them?

11. On page 188, Jo quotes Michele Guinness as saying, "If you are never criticized, you probably aren't changing anything." Do you agree? What would you need to change in your schedule to regularly "get feedback from someone you trust implicitly . . . [to] help you to grow, rather than crush your spirit"?

12. To what extent do you agree or disagree with what Jo Saxton is saying in this book? How has it challenged you?

13. How have others' insights in the course of discussion changed your perspective or understanding of anything from this book?

14. Having read *More Than Enchanting*, what would you like to do differently in the situations you lead or exercise influence?

15. Think of some women in your life who struggle with the issues discussed in *More Than Enchanting*. How can you encourage and empower them to fully embrace their influence?

16. Consider the various spheres in which you exercise influence. How can you make them more supportive of the free exercise of women's gifts?

About the Author

Jo Saxton is a pastor, missional leader, speaker, and author. She is the cohost of Lead Stories podcast and the board chair of 3D Movements. Jo previously authored *High Heels and Holiness* and *Real God, Real Life*. She lives in Minneapolis with her husband Chris and their two daughters.